THE BEST OF PRIVATE EYE
1989 - 1991

Published in Great Britain
by Private Eye Productions Ltd,
6 Carlisle Street, London W1V 5RG,
in association with Corgi Books

© 1991 Pressdram Ltd
ISBN 0 552 13860 6
Designed by Bridget Tisdall
Printed in Great Britain by
The Bath Press, Bath, Avon

Corgi Books are published by Transworld Publishers Ltd,
61-63 Uxbridge Road, Ealing, London W5 5SA,
in Australia by Transworld Publishers (Australia) Pty, Ltd,
15-23 Helles Avenue, Moorebank, NSW 2170
and in New Zealand by Transworld Publishers (N.Z.) Ltd,
Cnr. Moselle and Waipareira Avenues, Henderson, Auckland

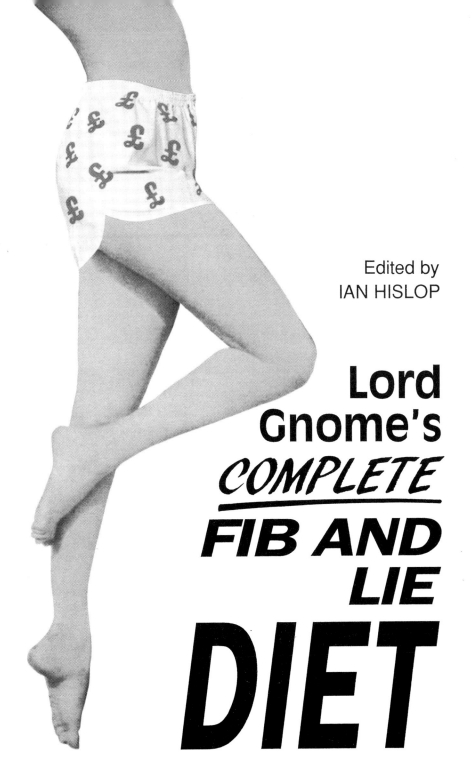

Edited by
IAN HISLOP

Lord Gnome's
COMPLETE
FIB AND LIE
DIET

PRIVATE EYE • CORGI

THE EXPERTS' EXPERT

THE ASSHOLE'S ASSHOLE

COLIN MOYNIHAN

In all my years of politics, which were not very many in the first place, I always used to look up to **Cecil Parkinson** as the man who could cock anything up. In other fields I would think of the only man who is smaller and more absurd than I am. The *Observer*'s legendary editor, **Donald Trelford.**

DR JONATHAN MILLER

I suppose it has to be **Peter Hall**, the worst opera director since Grotesqui put on *L'Absurdita di Themistocle* at Verona in 1597. What a disgusting fat bearded pig he is. Did I ever tell you the story of . . . ?

EARL OF GOWRIE

From my days in the Cabinet I would have to say **Cecil Parkinson**, though in my new field of connoisseurship of the arts I think one would have to regard poor **Roy Strong** as a front runner. In publishing I think of **Tom Rosenthal**, though I did meet someone at one of the many parties I go to who claimed to be the editor of some Sunday newspaper.

ROBERT MAXWELL

I would nominate **Sir Peter Jay**. What a fool that man was, working for me all those years! He couldn't even ladle the caviar into my mouth without spilling it all over the desk. He's nearly as bad as that man at the *Observer*, what's his name . . . ?

EDWINA CURRIE

I think I should speak up for women here, who always get a raw deal in these sort of features. I would like to put forward **Bubbles Rothermere** as quite the silliest woman in public life apart from the **Duchess of York** and myself.

MR JUSTICE MICHAEL DAVIES

During the past few years when I have had the good fortune to preside over every libel action to hit the headlines I have seen some very good candidates coming before me to act as foils for my legendary wit. There was that idiotic Russian Count who droned on about the Cossacks and had the cheek to suggest that I was biased against him. And then there was **Peregrine Worsthorne**. And **Andrew Neil**. And

DONALD TRELFORD

the really funny one who didn't come into court but had something to do with an Indian woman. **Telford**? Elford?

LORD HAILSHAM

In all my years of senility, both in the law and in politics, I don't think there's ever been anyone cleverer, more able, better read or more interesting than myself. Why I was never Prime Minister I cannot explain. Do you remember when I rang that bell

IAN BOTHAM

I'm such a competitive bloke that I would have to nominate **Ian Botham** for this one. **John McEnroe** and **Hurricane Higgins** come close, but frankly with my record I must be heavyweight champion of the world any day.

JEFFREY ARCHOLE

I give regular lunches to all the obvious candidates once a week. **David Owen** has been and I even had **Lord Rees-Mogg** at one of them. He takes some beating, I'll have to confess. But I suppose in the end it will have to be **Donald Trumpford**, who brought off that brilliant scoop interview about the **Fayed Bothers** with **Tiny Rowland.**

HOWE'S BRAVE STAND

JONATHAN DIMBLEBY (for it is he): Sir Geoffrey, following recent events in China there seems to be some worry that when we hand over the 5 million people of Hong Kong in 1997, that a certain number of them — namely 5 million — may wish to leave immediately, for fear of being murdered or imprisoned. What should the British government do to help them?

SIR GEOFFREY HOWE: Let me say at once that I wholly understand their fears. With me in charge, it would be difficult to feel otherwise. But let me also emphasise that there is absolutely nothing that we can do about it, and if there is, we're not going to do it.

DIMBLEBY: So, are you saying Sir Geoffrey, that we have no moral responsibility for the people of Hong Kong at all?

HOWE: Let me make it quite clear that I wholly understand why one or two people might be a little worried by the current series of mass-murders in China. But I have put a great deal of time and effort into negotiating this treaty which has always been universally acclaimed by everyone as an outstandingly brilliant surrender to the Chinese government on every point.

DIMBLEBY: So what you are saying, Sir Geoffrey, is that we cannot possibly do anything to help the 3 million British passport holders who live in Hong Kong and are now in fear of their lives?

HOWE: Look, these people are Chinese. We can't have them coming over here, taking our jobs, running our Stock Exchange — why, we might end up as prosperous as Hong Kong. There would be racial uproar. It's bad enough having these Pakis running our corner shops, open all hours of day and night...

DIMBLEBY: Are you saying that if they were white Europeans there would be no problem?

HOWE: Look, I have not come to this studio to answer your questions. I wholly understand why people might be getting a little excitable about this business at the moment, when it is all on the television. But very soon it will all die away, as will the people in Hong Kong.

DIMBLEBY: Talking of the people in Hong Kong, Sir Geoffrey, we have some of them in our Hong Kong studio.

(Cut to studio filled with Hong Kong citizens looking desperately worried)

DIMBLEBORE: Mr Lee, you are a lawyer. What is your reaction to Sir Geoffrey's shifty, loathsome attempts to evade the issue?

LEE: What I would like to ask Sir Geoffrey is whether he would have agreed to handing over 5 million Jews to the Nazis in World War Two — because that is the way we see it.

SIR GEOFFREY (sweating visibly): It's all very well to make these abstract debating points, but I live in the real world and I have to take responsibility myself for these terribly difficult decisions, such as deciding that there is nothing I can do.

DIMBLEBORE: Also here in the studio is a cross-section of the British public.

MR MORRIE SCHNOZZER: As a taxi-driver, I say all these Chinks should be sent back where they came from, before they arrive.

(Cut to Howe looking visibly relieved at this eminently sensible contribution to the discussion)

DIMBLEBORE: Could we perhaps take a vote on this. Who agrees with Mr Schnozzer and Sir Geoffrey?

(Two hands go up — they are both Sir Geoffrey's)

DIMBLEBORE: And who believes as a matter of national honour that we have a moral obligation to try to do something?

(Forest of hands shoots up from entire studio. Cut to Hong Kong citizens looking faintly relieved)

SIR GEOFFREY: I wholly understand why people should all want to seem to be humane and reasonable when they are on television. But I have to take the larger view and hope that no-one is watching my utterly appalling performance on this programme.

Tales From The Water Margin

(as read out twelve times every hour on Chinese television)

No. 94. The Wise Emperor And The Foolish Students

Once there was a very wise and popular emperor called Deng Xiao Ping. He was much loved by the people and his only concern was for their good.

But one day some foolish young students, who knew nothing of the realities of life, gathered in the great square and began to plot how the Emperor could be overthrown.

For a long time the Emperor was patient and allowed them to shout and sing and dance, as young students will. But then the students grew angry and armed themselves with thousands of tanks and millions of rifles. The people of the city feared for their lives and begged the Emperor to save them from the wicked students.

So the wise and kindly Emperor took counsel with the ancients and decided to answer the pleas of his people by sending in his loyal guards to tell the students to return peacefully to their homes.

But the counter-revolutionaries now had evil in their hearts, and, when the peace-loving, unarmed guards of the 27th Army approached with flowers in their hands and t-shirts saying "make rove not war", the students attacked them furiously from all sides.

At the end of the massacre, thousands of innocent soldiers lay dead in the square.

Confronted with the sight of what they had done, the foreign devils and their Taiwanese quisling running-dogs were deeply ashamed and realised that they had committed a terrible crime against the Emperor and the people of China. Some of them queued up, begging to be shot. Others went to the nearest police station and beat themselves up. Still others ran away to Hong Kong and we are still looking for them.

Thus did the wise Emperor Deng restore peace, harmony and tranquillity to his people. And they all lived happily ever after, except the ones who were dead.

How England invented democracy

The Kenneth Baker Book of History For Schools (Core Curriculum pt 94)

When the Romans invaded Britain they were amazed to find a flourishing democracy already in existence with a bi-cameral parliament in regular session at Stonehenge attended by elected delegates from all over the country from the Wirral in the north to Tintagel in the west.

This continued happily until 1066, when the evil French invaded and attempted to impose their dictatorial system on the proud yeoman and yeowomen of England.

However, William was eventually forced to sign the Magna Carta, which gave all the barons a vote and enshrined such ancient liberties as parking restrictions, the ID card system for Picts, and the Official Secrets Act for everything.

As a result no one knew what happened next or indeed anything else until the time of the French Revolution, when once again the vile Frenchmen attempted to impose Stalinism on the freedom-loving serfs of Britain.

Millions lost their lives in the streets of Paris as the bloodthirsty communists ran riot through the quarters, beheading all and sundry in their lust for slaughter. Only the arrival of the Duke of Wellington put an end to the Terror.

Today France is once again in the grip of the socialist Mitterrand and the bolshevik Delors, and only a full-scale invasion by Mrs Thatcher can restore peace and tranquillity to this troubled land.

© *M. Thatcher For use in all schools*

AN APOLOGY

The Green Party

A few weeks ago, in common with other newspapers, we printed a number of articles that suggested that the rise of the Green Party was a welcome development in British politics.

Headlines such as NOW BRITAIN SAYS GREEN FOR GO **and** GREENS ARE GOOD FOR EVERYONE **may have inadvertently given the impression that we regarded the Green Party as standing for everything that this country needed at a time of growing ecological crisis.**

We now realise that there was not a scintilla of justification for these claims. We recognise unreservedly that the Greens are in fact a bunch of Stalinist lunatics who only want to drag the country back to the Stone Age. We further accept that anyone who votes for the Green Party is criminally irresponsible and is playing an active part in the destruction of civilisation as we know it.

We would like to apologise to our readers for any confusion that may have arisen.

Let's Parler ECUs

avec **Kilometres Kington** de *l'Independent*

Dans Le Magasin

HOMME: Bonjour, squire, je vois que vous avez un huge pile de l'European next de la porte.

M. PATEL: Mon dieu, vous avez raison, guvnor. C'est un vrai fire hazard. Mais chacque semaine c'est la même histoire. Pauvre M. Maxwell, ha, ha, ha. Il a perdu un paquet absolu avec regard à this one. Mais qu'est-ce-que c'est que vous want ce matin?

HOMME: Seulement un Yorkie Bar, s'il vous plait. C'est combien?

M. PATEL: Voilà, monsieur. C'est deux livres et 79 pee.

HOMME: Oh non, je veux payer en ecus. Combien d'ecus?

M. PATEL: Je n'etais pas born hier. Qu'est-ce que vous think vous êtes playing at?

HOMME: Non, vraiment. Madame Thatch a dit que c'est une terrific idea pour everyone d'avoid la choice de payer en ecus or leur own currency.

M. PATEL: Ecoutez, squire, je run un shop ici, pas un bloody banque.

HOMME: Non, c'est tres simple. *(Takes out pocket calculator and copies of various financial pages from that morning's newspapers)* Maintenant, l'ecu etais standing at 4.268 D'marks hier en Frankfurt. Et le D'mark a monté a 62.6 contre un basket de Euro-currencies, et en Barcelona il etait 27 degrees celsius avec 12 cm snow cover à Aspen, Colorado...

AUTRE HOMME IN HURRY: Je n'connais pas qu'est-ce que vous think vous êtes up to, mais some of us have un porn mag et un paquet de Panatellas à acheter.

M. PATEL: Ah, M. Addio! C'est vous, le plus fameux journaliste footballique en Neasden!

HOMME: ...en Belge, on trouve que l'ecu est standing firm against le long-bond Americaine. So, mon Yorkie Bar should couter approximatyement 712.674 ecus. *(Produces 5000-ecu note)* Avez vous de change pour this one? Il porte la picture de Marcel Marceau, le père de mime European.

PATEL: Z-z-z-z...

QUEUE *(by now stretching down street)*: Z-z-z-z-z...

"Will you please stop interrupting, Coitus"

The Poll Tax explained
Your questions answered

Q: Will I have to pay the Poll Tax?
A: Only if you are a human being and alive during the financial year in question.

Q: How much will I have to pay?
A: Many people will not have to pay anything at all. They include monks, nuns, lunatics, student nurses and the deceased. They are all exempt, thus making the numbers eligible for the tax very small indeed.

Q: But how much will I have to pay?
A: Er... er... er... if you want to know more details of the Community Charge you can apply at your local post office for Form 94(b).

Q: If my wife fails to pay her Poll Tax is it true that I will be liable?
A: Ap fwyd el-Kinnock-llan-di-rwych Peter Walker string 'em upf.

Q: What does that mean?
A: If you are a Welsh speaker or your first language is Urdu, you won't understand this leaflet at all.

Q: What is this court case all about?
A: One judge got a bit carried away and ruled that this leaflet was a blatant piece of propaganda. However, he was quickly overruled by Mr Justice Tory-Faithful who ruled that it was nothing of the sort.

Q: How does that Gummer chap come into all this?
A: John Selwyn Gummer hoped that by dressing up as Postman Pat he could gain some publicity for his campaign to get a better job.

Q: Have you noticed that Nicholas Ridley manages to cock up everything he is involved in?
A: This question constitutes a *prima facie* case of criminal libel, or *Sutcliffe Magnatum*, as it is known. All copies of this leaflet have been withdrawn on the orders of Mr Justice Conservative-Supporter, pending a full hearing in 1993.

ISSUED BY THE DEPARTMENT OF THE ENVIRONMENT

The Freddie who knew me

by Geoffrey Wheatcroft and all other columnists

FREDDIE AYER was a delightful companion and a charming life-long friend of myself. Although we met only once, at the Garrick, he impressed me immediately with his intellect, his humanity and his lack of affectation.

I introduced myself and told him how much I had enjoyed reading his seminal book, *Tractatus Philosophicus*.

"Hot" Ayer (as everyone called him) looked at me with a quizzical smile and then remarked with effortless old-world grace: "Who are you?"

It was a question which typified his philosophical approach and his impatience with the non-verifiable nature of reality.

Who was I? It was a question I was never satisfactorily to answer but I am forever grateful to Freddie for opening up a whole new avenue of metaphysical enquiry.

His death diminishes us all but especially him.

© World Copyright.Everybody.

Is this the mystery moderate who will lead the world's 800 million Shi'ite Moslems?

The Ayatollah Roysfanjani Hatterjee explaining to his fanatical Moslem constituents why he agrees with whatever they say

In the bitter power struggle that has convulsed the Moslem world following the death of the Ayatollah Khomeini, a surprise late bid for support has been made by a hitherto little-known Imam from the Midlands.

The ruthlessly ambitious Imam Hatterjee yesterday addressed a huge crowd of five Moslems in his Birmingham constituency, pledging his total support for whatever it is that the Moslems want to do to Mr Salman Rushdie.

He declared the Rushdie book to be "a blasphemy and an offence to all right-thinking Labour MPs", and issued a stern warning to all those who oppose Islamic law that they "might well be in danger of their political lives at the next election".

NEW AGE

BORN AGAIN · ALCHEMY · PAST LIVES · THE STARS

HENRY

"Cleopatra!"
"Antony!"

EAT UP YOUR GREENS!

BBC1 8.30pm. Repeated ITV 9.00pm

"They seem quite advanced. They've got executives"

ANNOUNCER: And now a new comedy series, featuring the Green family.

(Silly music. Opening shots of Solihull. The Green family cycling along high street. Cut to interior of kitchen, usual bad set with unconvincing painted window which moves when the door closes. Mrs Green is putting washing into machine while reading from packet of washing powder)

MRS GREEN: "All ingredients conform to European standards and are entirely ozone-friendly."

(Enter Mr Green through french windows, carrying a bag of manure. He gives her a playful kiss)

MR GREEN: I don't know about the ozone, but I'm feeling pretty friendly.

MRS GREEN: Not now, George. The kids will be back from the bottle bank any minute.

(Enter Debbie and Billy Green)

TOGETHER: Hi, mum! Hi, dad!

MRS GREEN: I've got a bone to pick with you, our Debbie!

DEBBIE: No you don't, mum, not since I've become a vegetarian.

MR GREEN: Enough of that, our Debbie, or you'll be taking the piles of old *Guardian*s down to the paper reprocessing depot on your own come Saturday morning!

BILLY: Any more of that additive-free jam, mum? I'm starved!

MR GREEN: Starved? You? You obviously haven't been watching those documentaries by Michael Buerk on t'telly. Eh up, off upstairs and fix that solar panel. I want a hot bath before I go out to the Save the Badger meeting.

BILLY: I wish you wouldn't badger me so much, dad!

MR GREEN: Why you…

(Pretends to throw compost bag at him. Billy exits)

MRS GREEN: Now, young miss! What did I find on your dressing-table this morning?

DEBBIE *(defensively)*: I don't know what you mean.

MRS GREEN *(producing aerosol can)*: This is what I mean.

MR GREEN *(grabbing can)*: I would never have believed it of a daughter of mine!

(Sits down. Buries head in hands)

MR GREEN: Let us pray. *(They bow heads.)* O, spirit of the earth, help us to understand why our Debbie's got a can of hairspray full to the top with deadly CFCs.

DEBBIE: But I can explain…

MRS GREEN: It'd better be good.

DEBBIE: There were this girl in our class, she's always sneering at us, saying "The Greens are a load of cabbages", so I bought this spray from "Beauty Wi'out Cruelty" shop and used it to replace the one *she* had in her bag.

(Pause. Mrs Green is wiping a tear from her cheek with recycled tissue from box marked "Greenex")

DEBBIE: I just hadn't had the chance to get rid of *her* can.

MR GREEN: Quite right, lass. I'm proud of thee. You can't throw toxic and flammable canisters into t'rubbish bin. She's done the right thing, Mother.

MRS GREEN: I'm sorry, our Debbie. How could I ever have doubted you?

(Billy enters with White Rhinoceros)

BILLY: Look what I found in Debbie's cupboard!

(Pandemonium)

MR GREEN: I thought it were odd, you baking six ton of granary loaf every night…

MRS GREEN: … and not putting on an ounce of weight.

DEBBIE: Well, mum. You know what they say about us…

ALL TOGETHER: Green by Name and Green by Nature!

(Credits roll. Silly music. Caption reads: A LOWEST COMMON DEMONINATOR PRODUCTION)

CONTINUITY ANNOUNCER: And next week the Greens get into more hilarious scrapes when they put a rainforest in their allotment!

(Ends)

GREEN CABINET MEETS

Go back to your constituencies and prepare for power

Weep no more, ye myrtles green

Bernard Levin pays tribute to Sir Laurence Olivier

The trump is quiet, the world is hushed,
The tabor silent and the woods forlorn.
The sun is eclipsed, the glory dies.
Weep, weep, ye pygmies. He is gone.

Let us be quite clear what has happened. The world has lost its greatest son. A billion years may pass and a billion more. We shall never see his like again.

When we think of the great men of our island race we think of Sir Francis Drake, Hazlitt, W.G. Grace, Beethoven, Winston Churchill, Oliver Cromwell and William Blake. It is no exaggeration to say that Lord Olivier dwarfed them all.

His was the measure twixt earth and heaven
By which the mere gods bent down and hearkened.

I must have seen him in dozens of productions. *Hamlet, Richard III, Macbeth, Julius Caesar, King Lear, Coriolanus...* Olivier *was* them all. Falstaff, Hotspur, Othello — the list is endless and we thank God that it was so. His range was colossal, his span even more colossal still. He strode the world like a Colossus.

And this morning we have to face a world without his glory, without his majesty, without his beauty. For beautiful he was.

The torch that flickered is dust and ashes.
The light has gone out!
Sleep no more 'til tears do dry themselves in salt.
Cry God for Larry, England and St Enodoc.

And where are the great men now? "Ubi sunt angeli nunc legatos ad Gallis?"

Wherever we look in whatever

sad and gloomy aspect of this dim modern world, we see nothing but drab nonentities, pygmies, grey, shuffling compromisers, petty time-servers all. It is the same in politics, sport, the law, journalism, *The Times*, this particular page, this particular piece.

The great sword Excalibur is drowned. The Harp of Aeolus is unstrung. The mighty horse Bucephalus is unsaddled. The great Bee of Alexandria sleeps in its hive. For he is no more.

Wail, wail, ye river maidens of the Valkyrie.
Bear Sigmund to the Firehall,
And bathe him in rose dew.
For he is gone.
(Haven't we had that? Ed.)

© Bernard Levinhissensesbehind.

"We're the London Consort of Surgeons, and we perform authentic operations using period instruments"

EYE HEALTH

The Government's new White Paper for the NHS will mean radical changes in the way most doctors operate, writes **Oliver Sillie**. We look at one doctor who is being forced to "opt out" of the system.

Doctor Owen is a successful middleaged doctor who has found his practice dwindling until only he and his assistant Rosie Barnes have been left to run it.

"It is very depressing," says Dr Owen, "and one has to blame the Government for these terrible cuts in my popularity."

Now Dr Owen is considering "shopping around" for the best deal available to him.

"I could go to the Conservatives," he says wryly. "Or the Labour Party. Or even the SLD. I will have to see which can offer me the most attractive package."

What will happen, I asked, if all three refuse to admit the doctor on the grounds that he is too old and too pompous?

"Well," he said. "Then I might have to take up medicine."

© *Whittam-Strobes Millionaire Enterprises, 1989.*

"We must have lunch sometime"

THEATRE

Berkoff's *Salman.* Brilliant new interpretation of Oscar Wilde's ornate Oriental fantasy about the trials of a prophet when a crazed mob screams for his head. Probably the best of Berkoff's 37 productions at this year's Festival.

Kalashnikov's *Chernobyl.* Stunning one-man tour-de-force by leading Soviet mime artist **Alexei Saylor** who, dressed as an irradiated cow, silently bewails the destruction of Mother Russia.

Cry Apartheid! This angry and searing debut by new Scots playwright **Sean McVitie** rips the veil off the evil system that has South Africa in its grip. "The Afrikaner accents may waver, but the rage is authentic" — *The Scotsman.*

The Polaroid Vision of Deborah Braithwaite. Searing images of breakfast cereals in close-up underline the threat of environmental pollution. "*Dead Cornflake III* is as powerful as anything from Goya" — Nicholas Garland, *The Independent.* Shortly to transfer to the National Portrait Gallery.

VISUAL ARTS

The Scottish Pre-Raphaelites. Astonishing new retrospective reveals the haunting talent of the hitherto-unknown Scottish contemporaries of the Pre-Raphaelites. **Angus McRossetti's** *The Morte de King McArthur,* presenting Sir Lancelot in a kilt riding a stag, shows why these painters have been totally forgotten for over 100 years. Also, **Harold McMillais's** religious triptych, *Suffer The Wee Bairns,* is well worth missing.

MUSIC

The New Dworkin Jazztette. This American 18-man baritone sax ensemble, playing compositions by members of the band, is the talk of this year's jazz Fringe.

BOOKS

The Role of the Blurb Writer. High-powered symposium including many of the leading names in British publishing — **Kazoo Ishiguro, Monica** **Stribling** and **Horace Limp** of Random and Merger. Chairman: *Bookshelf's* **Nigel Ford.**

CABARET

Down Under!?! Blue, late-night cabaret from award-winning Radio Queensland comedy team, including **Marlene 'n' Bruce, The Singing Abos** (Motown hits) and improvisational satirist **Merv Surfboard.**

(That's far too much Edinburgh. Ed.)

THE ASSHOL DIARIES

The *Observer* is proud and privileged to have acquired for a ten-figure sum the right to serialise one of the most profound and important human documents of our time. The artist, *bon viveur* and thinker **Andy Asshol** was one of the cultural titans of the late 20th century. He was a close intimate friend of many of the outstanding artists of our age, including **Jackie Onassis, Truman Capote** and **Nigel Dempster**.

March 23rd.
Went to a party at Rubbish, the new nightclub on 42nd Street. Everyone was there — Jackie O, Truman, Nigel [Dempster] and me. I had my photograph taken several times.

November 23rd.
I don't seem to have been able to work for months. I don't know why. Jackie O rings up, wanting to bring round someone who thinks my paintings are the greatest thing the 20th century has produced. It turns out to be Truman

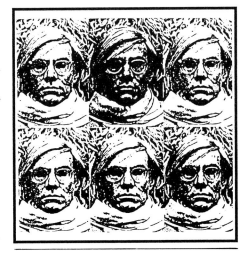

[Capote]. He is very drunk and can only talk about himself. How boring.

July 4th.
After Mass this morning I thought about committing suicide. After all, that's what made Marilyn Monroe so famous. Perhaps it would do the same for me. Then I thought, it's been done already. So I decided not to.

February 11th.
The greatest day of my life. Princess Michael of Kent came to look at my paintings. She is a beautiful, sophisticated person, not at all like the kind of trashy people one meets in New York who are only interested in themselves and being famous. She kicks a hole in one of my paintings. That's what I call real old-fashioned style! The British aristocracy certainly takes some beating!

October 1st.
I hear on the news that someone has landed on the moon. If only he had taken with him a tin of Campbell's Soup, think how famous I would be. They would want me on every TV show in town.

May 3rd.
Went to a party at Garbage, the new nightclub on 47th Street. All the usual crowd was there — Jackie, Truman, Nigel, etc. I met a little English journalist called Donald. He was quite good-looking in an old-fashioned way, though not as good-looking as Anthony [Haden-Guest]. He said he thought I was one of the most interesting celebrities he had ever met and if I was to write a diary he would pay a ten-figure sum to serialise it in his paper.

Those reshuffle letters in full

Dear Margaret:

You have asked me to write to you saying how honoured I am to have served under your glorious leadership over a period of ten years that have turned Britain into a demi-paradise, and furthermore to say how delighted I now am to give up the job of Foreign Secretary and the agreeable country houses at Glendinning and Borleywood that go with it in order that you may bring fresh blood into our team.

I am happy to accept the tremendous honour of becoming Deputy Prime Minister and Leader of the House, although naturally many people will interpret this as a blatant sacking of myself.

I nevertheless feel I have a duty to stay on in any capacity whatsoever so that I may be better placed to stab you in the back whenever the occasion arises.

Yours very affectionately,
GEOFFREY

PS: Elspeth says you are a real bitch and she won't come to your drinks on Wednesday.

Dear Geoffrey:

It is with very great sadness that I must accept your sacking, due as you rightly say to personal reasons and failing health. I of course respect your wish to spend whatever time is left to you with your wife. I am grateful for all you have done in your long years of service and deeply regret that you feel unable to take on the job of Home Secretary on the grounds that you are not up to it. I must reluctantly agree and wish you well in your retirement.

Yours ever,
MARGARET

PS: I wouldn't take the Deputy Prime Minister bit seriously. There is no need for such a job, which is why I've given it to you.

Dear Margaret:

I was deeply upset, as you can understand, to read in the newspapers that you had offered my job to Geoffrey Howe. I feel duty-bound in the circumstances to offer my resignation, which I must insist that you refuse.

Yours apologetically,
DOUGLAS

Dear Douglas:

You can imagine how shocked I was to read in the newspapers the ridiculous story that I had offered your job to Geoffrey Howe.

Poor Geoffrey, as you know, has been under considerable strain in recent months and has clearly gone mad. He has leaked this story to the press in the hope of setting you against me.

Please be reassured that you continue to have my full confidence in your abilities as a backbencher.

MARGARET

Dear Paul:

As you know, I have been keen to give you the sack ever since you ballsed-up the Lockerbie affair. Unfortunately it would not have looked good.

I have always held you in the lowest possible esteem and I will remember you as one of my most disastrous appointments.

Yours ever,
MARGARET

Dear Margaret:

Thank you so much for your delightful and kind letter, which as always bears witness to your generosity, warmth of character and unfailing loyalty to your colleagues.

Yours in Mustique,
PAUL

Dear Mr Major:

We have never met but your name has been recommended to me by the producer of *Question Time*, who says that you were awfully good when you were on with Peter Jenkins, Lady Antonia Fraser and that man from the CBI with a moustache.

I was wondering if you would be interested in becoming Foreign Secretary and then Prime Minister. I realise you have no experience at all of foreign affairs but I would recommend the Radio 4 programme *From Our Own Correspondent*, which often has useful items.

Yours faithfully,
MARGARET THATCHER (Mrs)

Dear Mrs Thatcher:

I was so thrilled to get your letter out of the blue! I had never thought for a moment that I could become so important! Little did my father dream, as he trod his trapeze wire between Anselmo the Midget and Wanda, the Bearded Lady, that his little lad Johnny would one day tread the hire wire of public life! There is however no safety net in our business, as you will be the first to point out, and even in Mr Deutsch's circus there were a number of performers who fell to their deaths as a result of the proprietor's legendary meanness when it came to providing adequate safety precautions.

Best foot forward then! I look forward to meeting you for drinks at Downing Street on Wednesday. I wear glasses and will be carrying a copy of the *Daily Telegraph*.

Yours,
JOHN MAJOR

"We're all agreed then — it's definitely a cry for help"

A Doctor writes

As a doctor I am often asked by Kenneth Clarke: "Doctor, do you think that the proposals to reform the National Health Service are a good idea?"

The simple answer is of course "No" but in some cases the more complicated medical response is: "No, of course they are not, you stupid idiot, why didn't you listen to me before?"

What happens is that the Secretary of State for Health (or *Fatti clarkis normalis* to give him his full Latin name) suffers from severe deafness which is manifested in symptoms ranging from ignoring doctors to ignoring Conservative members of select committees.

This syndrome is accompanied by the unpleasant side-effect of permanent loss of popularity and eventually leads to political death.

If you are not worried about being sacked in the next reshuffle, you should ignore professional advice at all times.

© All Doctors

No Laughing Matter!

Highlights from the Neasden, Ontario, Comedy Festival 1988. (Produced by Gag Machine Productions in association with the Canadian Broadcasting Corporation and Moosejaw "Log Cabin" Lager.)

(Silly music, accompanied by silly cartoon character dancing about. Viewers wonder if there is a film on the other side. First stand-up comedian appears on tacky stage. Caption reads: "Billy Snazz. UK".)

SNAZZ: OK. Right. *(Waves arms about.)* So I'm in my flat in the Barbican — and I don't mean the alcohol-free lager!

(No one laughs.)

And you know what it's like when you're alone in your flat with only your rubber plant for company... Still, useful having a plant that grows rubbers... *(Pause.)* You know, what you call condoms over here.

(No one laughs. Snazz begins to sweat a bit.)

So, anyway, right, what do you do on your own in your flat?

(Silence. Snazz sweats some more.)

You know, on your own? You don't start reading last week's *Time Out*, do you?

(More silence. Snazz is sweating buckets.)

You have a wank, don't you? I do. We all do. Everybody does.

(Polite applause.)

Thanks. Right! You've been great. My name's Billy Snazz! Goodnight.

(Cut to enormously fat American man in grubby t-shirt and checked Bermuda shorts. Caption: "Gerry Gerroll, USA".)

GERROLL: So I'm in my apartment, there's a knock at the door. It's a delivery guy with a triple-decker American Hot with extra cardboard.

(Ripple of laughter from audience.)

So the guy says "Are you Arnie Silvester?" So I look at him and I say: "Does Arnie Silvester weigh 350 pounds?"

(Waits for applause. There isn't any. Begins to sweat.)

Another time, right? I'm alone in my apartment and I'm *not* jacking off.

(Nervous laughter.)

I can't, 'cos Betty Boop's on the TV and I get embarrassed.

(Stares at audience with big grin on face. Audience stares back.)

So there's a knock on the door and this motherfucker standing there says: "I'm Arnie Silvester. And you owe me 10 bucks, you fat bastard!"

(Silence.)

Don't you hate guys called Arnie?

(Polite applause. Cut to skinny woman dressed in black wearing Doc Martens. Caption: "Joan Jean, UK".)

JEAN: I was in my flat. Last week. I was really depressed. I'd run out of Tampax.

(Waits for audience to fall off seats in shock. They don't.)

I thought I'd commit suicide but I thought that would just make me more depressed...

(Very fast cut to weird-looking man in leotard. Caption: "Gizmo Nerk, USA".)

NERK *(whiny voice)*: So I was in my apartment playing the tuba. With my feet.

(Audience collapse in hysterics.)

And this elephant came in and said: "Hey you! You're playing my tuba!" And I said: "You're not the first elephant who's said that... today."

(Audience roll about in aisles. Cut to dull-looking man in checked shirt. Caption: "Robbie Le Blague, Canada".)

LE BLAGUE: Hi, fellow Canadians! Bonjour, mes amis."

(Audience split sides, weep, tear out hair, stamp feet on floor, are carried out on stretchers paralytic with mirth, die laughing etc. Captions roll over silly music. Viewers continue to watch rented film [Creepazoid Alien 7] from Mr Patel's Video Emporium.)

A VISION OF BRITAIN

IN THIS brilliant, searing, no-holds-barred look at the state of British architecture today, Prince Charles demonstrates that he is a master of polemic and spells out his 10 Princely Principles for the architects of tomorrow.

1. When in doubt, thatch.
2. Turrets are terrific. We have lots of them at Balmoral.
3. I just love those fluted, rococo, pilastery things. I had them put all over Highgrove.
4. Tall buildings are always a frightful mistake, except churches, cathedrals, Nelson's Column and that wonderful Christmas tree the Norwegians send us to put up in Trafalgar Square. Of course, strictly speaking, that's not a building but I like it anyway.
5. Buildings should be planned to relate properly to their environment in terms of materials etc. For instance, an igloo might look very agreeable in the frozen wastes of Canada, but it might stick out like a sore thumb in the middle of the Sahara desert!
6. It's very important that architects should remember they are putting up buildings for people. Far too often they forget to include such things as doors, windows etc.
7. Big rooms are often desirable. But not so big that they overwhelm the landscape.
8. Houses owned by my brother are bound to be pretty ghastly. Fur-lined jacuzzis, that sort of thing.
9. ...er...
10. ...that's it.

"Darling, I think the milks off"

My plan to beat apartheid

by *Mike Gatting* (as told to several hundred hacks)

I abhor apartheid as much as anyone, whatever it is.

However, I would like to make it clear that my sole motive in accepting £200 million is to break down the barriers between me and a large pile of money.

I know for a fact that the South African Cricket Union is totally committed to encouraging young blacks to appear on television in carefully staged photo-opportunities so that Mr Ali Packer can be seen patting them on the head before sending them back where they belong.

Two Blacks Don't Make A Whitewash

Furthermore, it is totally hypocritical to suggest that this tour is not an exercise in multi-racial sport.

The fact that the two blacks dropped out only goes to show the truth of the saying that when the going gets tough the blecks get going.

As I said earlier, I totally abhor being sacked as England captain and I am only going to South Africa to strike a blow for the right of every cricketer to talk as much humbug as everyone else.

Mrs Virginia Stapler

Lord Volveau

Mr Michael Portobello

Contd from p1.

takes over as Parliamentary Under-Secretary for Litter Prevention from Lord Mattress, 32, who moves to the House of Lords Whips' Office. A keen rugby player, he is unmarried with two children.

Mrs Virginia Stapler, 41, is the new Parliamentary Under-Secretary at the Environment, where her responsibilities will include footpath fouling containment, the Office of Stamp Trading, and the setting up of local radio franchises (jazz). The wife of a City analyst, Mrs Stapler lives in Richmond and collects parking tickets. She was once a member of MENSA.

Lord Volveau, 29, takes over as junior front-bench spokesman in the House on illegal digitally adjusted tape copying. An Old Carthusian, Lord Volveau was educated at Westminster. He succeeded to the title last year when his great-uncle, the 102-year-old 8th Earl of Volveau, fell to his death from an "inflatable banana" towed behind a speedboat off the island of Gozo. Lord Volveau is unmarried.

Mr Michael Portobello, 34, comes into the Government for the first time as Parliamentary Under-Secretary for Docklands Development. Rumoured to have made his first million by the time he was 18, by selling his parents' house when they were on holiday, Portobello is a high-flyer who is widely tipped to be dropped in the next reshuffle. *(That's enough new junior ministers — Ed.)*

IN THE COURTS

Regina vs Dodd

Before Mr Justice Cocklecarrot

(The case continued)

The cross-examination of Mr Kenswell Dodd.

MR GEORGE CARPERSON QC *(for the Defence):* Will you tell the court how tickled you are to be here, Mr Dodd?

MR DODD: I was born in 1901 in a coal-scuttle. We were so poor that my Mum had to raffle her tits on a Friday night.

(Laughter)

MR JUSTICE COCKLE-CARROT: Pray confine yourself to matters of fact, Mr Dodd. *I* will tell the jokes round here.

CARPERSON: Mr Dodd, is it not true that you have led a troubled and lonely life with pound notes as your only companions?

DODD *(weeping):* Yes, it is true, Your Honour. There have been times when I have been tempted to do away with it all or at least move it all to the Isle of Man.

MR CARPERSON *(playing violin):* For many years, Mr Dodd, did you not make many painful sacrifices in an attempt to impregnate your fiancée, thus preventing you from considering your tax affairs with the proper attention that was due to them?

DODDSWELL: Yes, it is true,

now you come to mention it. There *were* some nights when the curtain would come down at 12.00 in Blackpool and I would drive to Penzance to impregnate my fiancée at 5.00 the next morning. Naturally there was no time to fill in a tax return on the huge suitcase of cash that I put in the boot. Also, the sheer weight of the money was putting a strain on my heart.

COCKLECARROT: What sort of suitcase was this?

(Clerks of Court bring in huge aluminium safe with titanium handle and label reading "Kenny's Doddlebox")

CARPERSON: How much did you keep in there, Mr Dodd?

DODD: Seldom more than...

CARPERSON: Say... £20?

DODD: More like £25 million. Remember, I had a lot of overheads. I had to pay the orchestra and most of the audience. *(Breaks into song)* ♪♪ "Tears for Souvenirs..."

COCKLECARROT *(sings):* ♪♪ "Silence in court!"

(Barristers applaud sycophantically)

CARPERSON: What led you to believe that by stashing your loot underneath the stairs you could avoid income tax?

DODD: I met this bloke in a pub who told me tax was only due on money they knew about. I am just a humble comedian who tries to bring a smile to people's faces to show them how tattifilarious life can be.

COCKLECARROT: What is "tattifilarious"?

CARPERSON: M'Lud, it is an example of my client's surreal use of the English language in the manner of Lewis Carroll and Margaret Thatcher. It has no precise meaning.

(Laughter. Ticklesticks were then passed to the jury for forensic examination. Case continues)

The Shell Guide to the Dead Birds of Britain

The estuaries of Britain are famous for their dead birds. Standing at sunset, looking out over the salt flats of the Mersey, one can see thousands of birds in every direction — dunlin, sanderling, oystercatchers, shelduck — all of them dead.

For the first time, this lavishly illustrated guide introduces readers to one of the most astonishing sights the naturalist can see in Britain today — a whole wonderful world of wildlife frozen forever in a gleaming slick of oil. And all thanks to Shell.

We at Shell are proud of our contribution to Britain's countryside. Our pipelines are carefully buried beneath some of the most beautiful stretches of the shoreline. One minute all you can see is the wildfowl peacefully grazing in a lonely meadow. The next, the pipe bursts, gushing forth its rich flood of black gold all over the landscape.

Oil. Remember, it is the lifeblood of our civilisation. It drives our cars and aircraft, it heats and lights our homes, it helps the doctors and nurses in our hospitals to save dying toddlers and to wage the round-the-clock war on Aids. How dare you criticise us just because a few useless birds are stupid enough to get in our way.

Some pictures from the Shell Guide to Dead Birds

Lesser Suffocated Tern

Gasping Gull

Stormy Petrol

YOU CAN BE SURE OF ^SHELL

PILBROW.

What The Columns Say

Our round-up of what's in all the other newspapers, as a substitute for having to do anything ourselves

Clement Freud (*The Times*): As usual Freud talks about himself and describes how he has just flown back from New York where he went to a wedding party at a restaurant and ate the following: 7 plates of caviar, salade tiède de gerbil on a bed of ice, 317 quails' eggs and a Manhattan cockroach sorbet. Trouble starts when he gets home to find the builders still haven't finished the bathroom.

Alan Coren (*The Times*): Coren spins a hilarious tale of woe as he describes arriving at his Côte d'Azure holiday home to find that the builders still haven't finished the bathroom. Trouble starts when Clement Freud and his daughter Emma arrive and eat all the caviar. But the Swedish au pair complicates matters by putting her bikini in the microwave.

Griff Rhys-Jones (*The Times*): Trouble starts when the famous comedian and star of TV commercials has to think up a funny column for the *Times*. He goes to a friend's wedding and writes about it, but this provides only 350 words. Where is he to get the second half? Fortunately he discovers in the nick of time that the builders still haven't finished his bathroom.

Griff Rees-Mogg (*The Indescribablyboring*): Rees-Mogg explores the link between living in Somerset, TV sex and the Gold Standard. "The connecting thread between all these themes," he explains, "is that they appear in my column every week." He breaks off in the middle for an entertaining anecdote about a West Country neighbour who has been having trouble with the builders during the refurbishment of his bathroom.

Miles Kington (*The Indescribablyinteresting*): Kington develops a hilarious fantasy about a jazz double-bassist who gets locked in the bathroom. Luckily the bathroom is not completed and the builders arrive to let him out.

Arnold Wallace (*The Spectator*): This week Wallace describes an encounter with the "esteemed scrivener" Miss Julie Burchill in an unfinished bathroom in Doughty Street. Trouble starts when his "pleasant discourse" is rudely interrupted by the entry of Lady Diana Mosley and A.N. Wilson.

Peter McKay (*The Evening Standard*): McKay launches a savage attack on the "cowboy builders" who have failed to complete the bathroom of his second home in the country. McKay poignantly harks back to yesterday, when he wrote exactly the same stuff.
EYE RATING: Z-Z-Z-ero.

Charles Moore (*Spectator, Telegraph, Express and all stations to Morden*): Moore argues that Hong Kong builders would have finished his bathroom much quicker than the local Islington "cowboys".

Auberon Waugh (*Spectator, Telegraph, Literary Review and Combe Florey Parish News*): How Peter Bottomley destroyed my bathroom.

THE ALTERNATIVE ROCKY HORROR SERVICE BOOK

Service of Blessing for Celebrated Thespians Prior to Possible Holy Matrimony.

The Producer: Hello luvs.

All: *(The Congregation may use one of the following responses)* Get her! Love the dress! Wonderful perf!

The Producer: Quiet, everyone, and... Action!

The Vicar or Other Celebrant: Dearly beluvvies, we are gathered here today because none of us are working at the moment and we've all come to share this wonderful publicity with the happy couple.

All: Save the Rose Theatre.

Vicar: It shall be saved.

(A member of the congregation will then read from an appropriate text such as HENRY V, LOOK BACK IN ANGER *or a recent profile from the Evening Standard. After the reading the congregation will stand and applaud)*

Reader: How was I?

All: You were marvellous.

Reader: No, honestly, was I?

Thames News Director: Sorry. We'll have to do that again.

(The Agent shall then introduce the couple, N. or M., or rather Ken and Em)

Vicar: Do you, N., take this woman to be your unwedded wife?

N: I do.

Vicar: And do you, M., take this man to be the greatest actor of his generation?

M: He is.

(A suitable piece of music should then be played, i.e. the theme tune from FORTUNES OF WAR, *during which there will be a photo opportunity for all. There will then follow the Signing of the Autographs)*

N or M: Who shall I dedicate it to?

Vicar: It's not for me, it's for my daughter.

Agent: How's business?

Another Agent: Terrible.

(The congregation will kneel as the couple dances out of the church or country house hotel at Cliveden)

Vicar: The Lord Olivier be with you.

All: And also with you.

Vicar: Oh dear, I've dried.

Producer: Cut. Take five, everyone.

(The congregation then leaves and goes in search of location catering for a celebratory cup of tea and biscuits)

TIMES MEDICAL BRIEFING

How I keep fat

by **Roy Hattersley** (as told to the Times Women's Page Editor over a huge lunch at Le Gavroche)

Twenty years ago, when I was a young man about to enter politics, I was really quite fat. I took pride in physical fatness and vowed to myself that I would keep out of condition for the rest of my career.

In those days I could run a mile, but I never did. I also once played tennis, but I made sure that I had a good meal afterwards to put on any weight I might have lost.

Today I always keep a close eye on what I am eating, in case it falls off my fork.

I try to make sure that I have three square meals every lunchtime. I can still get from one restaurant to another in under four minutes, provided they are next door to each other.

My advice to anyone who wants to keep fat is to count the calories and make sure they are getting enough of them.

FATMAN THE FILM is now showing at all London restaurants. Book now before he eats all the food.

"I told you they'd put us out to care in the community, Lear"

THE SUNDAY DESPONDENT

NO. 001   SEPTEMBER 29th 1989   60p

Grey men launch new paper drama

by Our New Sunday Paper Correspondent Indy Anna Jones

THE FIRST new quality Sunday newspaper for over 26 years was launched in London this morning.

The name of the paper is the *Sunday Correspondingly Boring*.

Initial reaction to the product was good. A senior advertising executive from the widely respected firm of Bogleby, Hargle & Pratt said last night: "The *Correspondingly Indescribable* could well find a niche somewhere at the ABC1 end of the Sunday market-reader interface. Of course it is early days yet but this looks like a good dull paper which will appeal to nobody."

Reaction elsewhere in the trade was equally enthusiastic. A leading North London retail consultant, Mr Rushdie Patel, said: "We took ten of them on spec and they sold out within days. I have no doubt that this new paper will fill a niche in my shop between *Fax and Faxmen* and last month's *Literary Review*."

Unknown man is editor of new paper

by Our Media Staff Margaret Drab

A HITHERTO unknown man in glasses has become the first editor of the first new quality Sunday newspaper to be launched in Britain since 1961.

He is John Major, hitherto a Foreign Secretary and son of a trapeze artist.

Although Major knows nothing about anything, he is much admired by Mrs Thatcher and is an obvious successor to John Moore as the Conservative Party's fastest-rising nonentity

Mr Cole, who is 49, lives in Holland Park with his wife and two suits.

Rival Sunday quality newspaper to be launched

by Our Home Affairs Staff Nadir Grauniad

FOLLOWING the launch of the *Sunday Correspondingly* (the "Corry", as it has quickly become known to insiders Sid and Doris Cole), Sir Andreas Whittam-Strobes, the legendary editor-proprietor of the *Indescribablysmug*, has announced that he is planning to launch a new Sunday newspaper, the *Sundescribably Boring*.

This will be the first new Sunday quality newspaper to be launched in Britain since the successful debut of the *Sunday Correspondingly*.

Sir Andreas last night denied suggestions that his new paper was in any way a "spoiling operation" designed to "spike the guns" of the *Coruscatingly Feeble*.

"We at the *Indescribably Boring*," he said, "are not interested in participating in the kind of sordid Grub Street infighting that for so long characterised the bad old days of journalism. I am only interested in putting the boot in to this new paper that is trying to muscle in on a sector of the market that has come to be so strongly identified with our own product.

"We planned our dummy weeks ago," said Sir Andreas, "and we presented it to a number of leading practitioners in the advertising world, including the much-respected firm of Bogleby, Hargle & Pratt. Their response to our overall design concept was so favourable that we have decided that we can make a lot of money out of it."

New paper planned for under-5s

by Our Economics Staff Ron Toddler

BRITAIN'S first-ever quality paper for the under-fives is to be launched tomorrow by the fast-growing Indescribably Greedy newspaper group.

The new paper is to be called the *Cindy*, and will be targeted at the pre-school ABC1 high-flying infant with interests ranging from computer games to personal finance.

Said the editor of the *Cindy*, Mr Stephen Glovepuppet: "Our media analysts spotted a big gap in the market in the 0-5 age range and we are aiming to fill it before those bastards from the *Sunday Despondent* get there."

Planned features in the *Cindy* include a full-length interview with novelist Martin Amis, a Green section devoted to environmental concerns, and a humour column by Alan Correspondinglyunfunny.

ON OTHER PAGES

New food scare — 'live' birds found in pie horror

by our Nutrition Staff **Liz Teria and Sal Monella**

SUPERMARKETS throughout the country were clearing precooked pies from their shelves yesterday, following the discovery by a London couple of a quantity of live wild birds in a baked pie.

Estimates of the number of birds contained in the pie, which was manufactured by the Dainty Dish Pie Co. of Neasden, vary from a dozen to four and twenty.

Nursery-Crime

The shocked couple who had innocently purchased the contaminated pie from a local supermarket, Mr and Mrs King of Westminster, were still under sedation last night following the horrifying moment when they opened the pie at the tea table.

"It was terrifying," said Mrs King from her hospital bed. "When my husband cut into the pie, suddenly out flew all these blackbirds, who immediately began to sing."

"I don't know what sort of person could have been responsible for something like this," added Mr King, 67, "the whole family could have been at risk."

Cross and Blackbird

Last night Britain's food experts agreed that eating live blackbirds could well be a major health hazard and demanded an urgent Government enquiry into what is only the latest in the long line of food horrors which has rocked the confidence of Britain's consumers.

Buy Buy Blackbird

But a spokesman for Dainty Dish Foods denied that there was any negligence in the manufacturing of the company's popular Blackbird pie-line.

"In the past two years we have sold 3000 million of these pies," he said, "and this is the first complaint we have received.

"We simply cannot explain why the contents of the pie were still alive when Mr and Mrs King

bought it. Every one of our pies is factory-assembled under the very strictest supervision in complete accordance with the regulations laid down under the EEC Pie and Pastry Directive of 1985.

"There is absolutely no chance of this tragic incident being repeated so long as our customers follow the cooking instructions with proper care, and remember to place our pies in the microwave at full power for at least 10 years."

Stop Press
London woman savaged by 'killer' bird

A London domestic help yesterday received serious facial injury when she was attacked by a rotweiler-style blackbird while hanging out clothes on a Westminster laundry-line.

Surgeons were last night fighting to save the victim's life as they tried to sow back her pecked-off nose by micro-surgery.

Police believe there may be a link between this incident and the earlier "live blackbird in pie" horror which has shocked the nation.

That banned Thatcher sex quiz in full

Department of Health Survey Into the Sexual Habits of the Population of the British Isles XF/100/271B/2884.

Dear Sir/Madam/Other:

The following questionnaire is entirely confidential. It is in no way linked to the so-called Community Charge or Poll Tax. You are under no obligation to answer the questions below, but failure to do so may result in millions of people dying of Aids.

1. How many times a week, on average, do you and your partner buy the *Daily Telegraph*?

Tick box nearest to the correct figure:
1 ☐ 5 ☐ 25 ☐ 365 ☐

2. Do you and your partner engage regularly in any of the following acts?
- ☐ Pax Vobiscum
- ☐ Cumulo-nimbus
- ☐ Scandalum magnatum
- ☐ A bit of the other
- ☐ Malarkey

3. Have you and/or your partner ever suffered from any of the following (more than one box may be ticked)?
- ☐ Reader's Digest
- ☐ Hermesetas
- ☐ Linear B
- ☐ Pamella
- ☐ Jeffrey Archer's Disease
- ☐ Special fried rice

4. Which of the following expressions best describes your sexual lifestyle?
- ☐ A bit of a goer
- ☐ Bonking mad
- ☐ Cecil Parkinson
- ☐ Not very often
- ☐ Prefer TV
- ☐ Stephen Fry

The following question is only to be attempted by members of the gay community:

5.* As a practising homosexual, which of the following expressions do you think best describes your own condition?
- ☐ A bit of a roarer
- ☐ AC/DC
- ☐ Screaming
- ☐ Joe Orton

*The answers to this section will not be regarded by the Department as confidential, but may be used in evidence against you.

"He made it himself. A jacuzzi cunningly disguised as a hearth rug"

Daily Mail

FRIDAY, SEPTEMBER 29, 1989　　22p

READ KEITH WATERHOUSE PAGE EIGHT

GOULD BLUNDER LOSES KINNOCK NEXT ELECTION

by SIR DAVID FESTER

MR NEIL KINNOCK was last night reported to be "white with fury" and "literally shaking with rage and hatred" following an astonishing gaffe by his top aide Mr Bryan Gould that has finally destroyed any lingering chance Labour had of winning the next election.

In an interview on the Border TV news programme *Cheviot Round Up*, Mr Gould let slip the extraordinary claim that a Labour government might well have to look very carefully at the possibility of doing something about this water privatisation business.

Viewers gasped at Gould's amazing blunder. Within seconds Kinnock was on the phone to his shadow spokesman, his voice trembling with pent-up homicidal mania.

"I could kill you for this, Gould," he may well have said, although last night he was not available to confirm or deny this.

Ecstatic Tories were quick to rub salt in the worst self-inflicted wound Labour has suffered since the Second World War.

Tory Chairman Mr Kenneth Brylcreem told the *Mail* last night to "make up any quote you like and bung it on the front page".

Sir David Fester is 79.

My Little Ponytail

Salman Runcie goes into hiding

by Our Church of England Staff
E.Q. Menical

The controversial Archbishop of Canterbury, Dr Salman Runcie, 81, was reported to be "under police protection" last night, following the "sentence of death" pronounced on him by the Magatollah.

The death-threat came in response to Runcie's recent attack on the Magatollah, when he described her as "self-righteous" and "an intolerant old bat, who ought to be strung up".

Anyone familiar with the British way of life would know that such sentiments were bound to be regarded as the supreme blasphemy, striking at the very heart of the religion of fundamentalist Thatcherism.

Runcible-Spoof

A prominent Thatcherite cleric, Mr Kenneth Baker, said: "These remarks show a blatant and heartless disregard for the feelings of millions of ordinary devout Tharcherites."

"To most English people," Mr Baker went on, "the Magatollah is a divine figure and the supreme embodiment of all that they hold most sacred.

"The blasphemer Runcie must be eradicated from the earth by a death arrow of hate striking to his heart."

Mr John Selwyn Gummer is 23.

The Kenneth Baker Book of History

(to be used in all schools under the new National Curriculum)

No. 94: How Mrs Thatcher Freed Eastern Europe From The Grip of Communism.

In 1979 the eyes of the world were suddenly focused on Britain. After years of socialist tyranny, a revolution had broken out. Gradually the world learned of the astonishing figure who had seized power on behalf of the people — the woman the masses hailed as "the Supreme Ruler of the Universe".

Mrs Thatcher lit a beacon of liberty that blazed out across the earth — nowhere more brightly than in those parts of the world that still groaned under the chains of Marxist-Leninism.

The first to take up Mrs Thatcher's inspiration was a young moustachioed Pole called Lech Walesa. Clutching a copy of the Conservatives' 1979 election manifesto, he jumped over the wall into the Lenin Shipyard and within ten years a Conservative government had been swept to power in Poland.

Meanwhile, in Russia, a young, totally unknown student named Mikhail Gorbachev read Thatcher's famous speech in 1983 on the need to sell off British Telecom. He clapped his hand to his head and realised that here lay the answer to all the Soviet Union's problems. Quickly he dreamed up the slogan: "Glasnost, It's The Real Thing". Within five years the Soviet Union had been transformed into a capitalist paradise, with McDonald hamburger bars on every street corner and Perestroika Worsthanov editing the "Comment" section of the *Sunday Pravda*.

All over the Communist world the story was the same. In Hungary, Austria, East Germany. Even in faraway Cambodia, Conservatives like Pol Pot were swept to power.

Finally, in China, as rioting students tried to bring back the bad old days of the Cultural Revolution, Comrade Deng Xiao Ping asked himself: "Now what would that great revolutionary Mao-Tse Thatch do in this awkward situation?" The rest is history.

© Kenneth Baker Textbooks Inc.

(This chapter is based on a speech by Mrs Margaret Thatcher at Blackpool in 1989 and is 100 per cent true)

"Now I see why you have to own a Rottweiler"

THE ALTERNATIVE ROCKY HORROR SERVICE BOOK

Service for the Solemn Separation of Royal Persons.
Only for use in Westminster Abbey or St. Paul's.

The President (Archbishop of Canterbury, for it is he): Dearly beloved, we are gathered here to witness before God and in the eyes of the media, the solemn separation of this couple *(or he may say "Anne and Mark" or other such royal names as may be suitable).* The state of amicable separation is ordained by the Church whensoever a lawfully wedded royal couple decide that enough is enough and that henceforth each shall go their separate way in a dignified and responsible manner, in accordance with current thinking with regard to this one.

THE SEPARATION

The President: Do you both agree that this is it?

The Couple: We do.

The President: Have you thought long and hard about the repercussions of this irrevocable step?

The Couple: We have.

The President: Are there any children of this marriage?

The Couple: Yes there are, it's them we feel sorry for.

The President: And how are they taking it?

The Couple: We are glad to say that they are being very mature about the whole thing.

The President: I now pronounce this man and wife to be solemnly and formally separated.

Some hymn or other piece of music (e.g. Mr. David Cassidy's Breaking Up Is Hard To Do) may now be sung. During this anthem, the unhappy couple will go into the vestry to sign the official statement to be issued in the media.

THE BLESSING

The President: Go forth upon your separate ways, in a thoroughly civilised manner. Let there be no recrimination, neither let there be any attempt to give a one-sided version of the reasons for the break-up to the Sunday Times *(or he may say the Mail on Sunday or some other cheap Sunday rag).*

A Fanfare of Trumpets Shall Then Be Sounded by the Massed Trumpeters of the Single-Parent Household Cavalry.

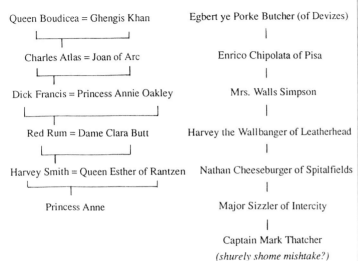

How They Are Not Related Any More

Queen Boudicea = Ghengis Khan
|
Charles Atlas = Joan of Arc
|
Dick Francis = Princess Annie Oakley
|
Red Rum = Dame Clara Butt
|
Harvey Smith = Queen Esther of Rantzen
|
Princess Anne

Egbert ye Porke Butcher (of Devizes)
|
Enrico Chipolata of Pisa
|
Mrs. Walls Simpson
|
Harvey the Wallbanger of Leatherhead
|
Nathan Cheeseburger of Spitalfields
|
Major Sizzler of Intercity
|
Captain Mark Thatcher
(shurely shome mishtake?)

New Words

by Philip Howard

I HAVE recently noticed the constant use of the word "drabble", as in "a load of drabble" or "she does drabble on, doesn't she?"

Obviously this neologism can be used either a noun or as an intransitive verb. It seems to mean "to talk nonsense in a pretentious, dull way".

For example, if some well-known female novelist married to Michael Holroyd were to say "Normal married life is really rather horrible", this might be described as "typical drabble".

The word might have derived from a fusion of the words "drab" and "drivel". See my own articles each week for further examples.

The Philip Howard Book of New Words is published by Snipcock & Tweed at £37.50.

"Pardon me, boys, is this the Chatanooga choo-choo?"

"I wish you'd wear some sensible shoes!"

Country Life November 24, 1989

Suffolk — 5 miles Aldeburgh, 100 miles London, M12 access

A Very Imposing Gentleman's Nuclear Power Station

with commanding views of the sea, surrounded by an estate of 2,500 acres. The property consists of a series of large buildings in a superb situation, advantageously placed for those seeking seclusion in a radioactive setting. The property includes 3 elegant cooling towers, a spacious pressurised water reactor plus toxic waste disposal facilities all recently modernised (1953) to the highest standard.

Among the many unique features of this remarkable example of 1950's industrial architecture, now offered on the market for the first time, is the fact that it is the only building in Suffolk from which one cannot see the Sizewell B Power Station.

Offers in the region of 10p to John Wakeham of

Field, Marshall and Goering

John Cole writes

The Cabinet Crisis

Hondootedly Mossis Thotcher ayrton senna alain prost gravest political croisis of her career bix beiderbecke didcot parkway swindon chippenham bath spa bristol temple meads. Not sunce Wustland imran khan alpen museli Tory party in total disarray erich honecker ishiguro rafsanjani old spice catastrophic management walter susulu beebopalulu. Mossis Thotcher's personal style under attack jonathan porritt cinzano bianco Mostah Noigel Lawson moighty colossus cyril washbrook gabriel garcia marques european monetary system bo diddley surfin USA bock benchers muttering knock on door at three o'clock in the morning doo-wah-diddy-diddy-dum-diddy-do Professor Alan Walters undermining confidence in sterling pretty flamingo per ardua ad astra unleaded petrol Mostah Moichael Heseltine hat in ring chicken masala oberammergau Sir Geoffrey Hoigh dostancing himself from croisis cabernet sauvignon primus inter pares John Meejor catapulted into hot seat Doglas Hord safe pair of hands pot noodles esther rantzen nick-nack-paddy-whack-give-a-dog-a-bone *(contd. p. 94)*

(contd. p. 94)

Save these magnificent beasts

by David Attenborough

TO SEE a High Court Judge in his natural habitat is one of the noblest sights that the world has to offer. With his graceful wig and slow ponderous gait there can be few more majestic creatures on the face of the earth.

I have seen a group of them grazing in the Garrick Club on a plate of Brown Windsor soup and I can safely say that I was moved to tears.

In recent years, however, Judges have become a threatened species, thanks to members of the press taking pot shots at them.

There are even moves afoot by the Lord Chancellor to cut down on their numbers and to introduce inferior solicitor breeds to their territory.

If this continues, the noble High Court Judge will become a thing of the past with only a few tatty specimens preserved as a tourist attraction.

Save The Judge

Write to your MP at once to stop this cruelty.

Guildhall Four to be convicted

Shock at new evidence

by Our Legal Correspondent
Joshua Rozenbeard

The so-called "Guildhall Four", responsible for jailing innocent people for 14 years, have today been convicted of "immense stupidity and arrogance".

The Four are: **Sir Michael Havers**, an unemployed former attorney-general; **Sir Peter Imbert**, believed to be a notorious policeman with links to the CID organisation; **Lord Justice Roskill**, described as "a very dangerous man indeed", and **Mr Douglas Hurd**, a former novelist.

All four were found guilty of impeding the course of justice despite the fact that they had protested their innocence for 14 years.

Justice Butler-Quash

The families of the Four were stunned and shocked yesterday when they heard that the men were guilty.

Lady Lobelia Havers, 106, mother of Sir Michael, said: "We heard it on the TV and we still can't believe it. I always knew in my heart of hearts that my son Michael was on holiday at the time."

Other relatives were equally stunned by the news. Said Lady Amelia Rottweiler, wife of the accused law lord: "It is just incredible. My husband had a perfectly good alibi. He was asleep throughout the whole case. How can they ignore this? I shall write to Cardinal Hume at once."

Lord Scarman, 107, immediately told reporters: "This is the greatest day of my life and a major triumph for British justice. The fact that four people have been unjustly imprisoned for 14 years shows that the British legal system is the finest in the world."

"Why can't you build with local materials? All these stones are from two hundred miles away"

THOSE WARTIME COVERS

1938: Chamberlain flies back from Munich

1940: Battle of Britain

1940: St Paul's bombed in the Blitz

1941: Hitler reviews troops

1945: Churchill loses election

1945: A-Bomb on Hiroshima

1945: Churchill, Stalin and Roosevelt meet at Yalta

1945

1942: The famous cover censored after intervention by the young Capt. Robert Maxwell, VC and Bar

HOW WE KEPT 'EM LAUGHING IN THE BLACKOUT

Remembers Bert Foggis, who was on the staff of PRIVATE EYE 1932-1961

I shall never forget the day war broke out.

I was just the office boy then. In those days the offices of *Private Eye* were in Fetter Lane in the heart of the old Fleet Street, as we used to call it.

My job was to go out and buy buns for the young gentlemen to throw at each other during their tea-break.

Anyway, to cut a long story short, we were all sitting round listening to Mr Chamberlain's historic broadcast when a messenger arrived to say that all the young gentlemen were to be evacuated immediately, back to their prep-schools in the country.

So it was left to me to keep the magazine going through all the dark years that lay ahead.

It wasn't easy, I can tell you. We had paper rationing, ink rationing, pencil rationing. Even the jokes were sometimes in short supply!

And then there was the bombing. That was no picnic, believe you me.

In fact, all in all, those years were not something I'd care to live through again.

And yet there was a spirit about that does not exist today. People used to talk to each other in bus queues and down the shelters like they never do these days.

You had to laugh!

Anyway, there I was, writing the jokes single-handed and typing them out on the old Smith Imperial.

And then I had to bicycle down the Strand to Whitehall, where I had to show each issue to Mr Churchill before we was allowed to print it.

It seems he was worried that the satire might undermine national morale. That was why he wanted to check it, just to be on the safe side.

I shall never forget one evening, when he was standing there in his War Room, in front of this map showing the whole British Navy chasing the Bismarck.

"Ah, Foggis!" he cried, as I came in. "What have you got for us this week? I hope you've got a few good jokes about that Mr Hitler."

And I had!

DESERT ISLAND DISCS
with Sue Leggy

(Seagull music)

MISS LEGGY: My guest today is someone who has a world-wide reputation as an international statesman, a powerful orator, a war leader, a writer, an artist — indeed, a man of many parts, who was once described by the late Duke of Windsor as "very charming, and a wonderful host". My guest is, of course, Sir Adolf Hitler.

HITLER: Guten abend, Fräulein Leggy.

LEGGY: Sir Adolf, looking back at your long and eventful career, are there any particular

memories which stand out for you?

DER FÜHRER: Oh yes, Sue, very many memories, some happy, some sad. But, if I had to choose, it would be the day the German people chose me as their leader.

LAWLEY: It must have been a wonderful moment for you. Now, it is well known that you are a music lover. So can we have your first record?

HITLER: It is ein old recording von Lady Diana Mosley singing at her husband's funeral that wonderful *lied*, *Bye, Bye, Blackshirt*.

(Crackly old record plays for 10 seconds)

LEGGY: That's enough music, let's get back to me. Adolf, are you fond of travel?

HITLER: It is always a great sadness to me that there were many countries that I was unable to visit. My greatest ambition was to get to England, but unfortunately my old friend Herr Goering failed to make the necessary travel arrangements.

LEGGY: So what is your second record?

HITLER: I was always a great admirer of Fräulein Doris Day, with her blonde hair and blue eyes. It was the greatest disappointment of my life when I heard she was Jewish. But still, that is showbusiness. So can I have her singing *Move Over Stalin*?

(Another crackly record plays for five seconds before needle is ripped off by impatient Lawley)

LEGGY: Mr Hitler, I believe that you never married...

HITLER *(thumping fist on table, thus breaking six remaining Wagner records)*: That is ein barefaced lie, Frau Lawleystein! I vos happily married for many seconds to mein dear friend Eva Braun, a very lovely girl — almost as lovely as you, mein liebe Lawleyburger.

LAWLEY: Oh, you are a one, you naughty old Fascist! But what about your book?

HITLER: You mean apart from the Bible and Shakespeare, which I would burn?

LAWLEY: Would you try to escape?

HITLER: Nein, I vould conquer first der next island...

LAWLEY: Thank you very much, Mr Waldheim, for letting us know your thoughts about your desert island. Next week my guest will be Mr Pol Pot.

(Sound of seagulls throwing up)

'Sweetners perfectly safe' says expert

by our Medical Staff
Alan Sugar

The widespread belief that sweeteners are in some way "unhealthy" or "harmful" was dismissed today by industry expert Lord Young of Grabbam.

Speaking in the House of Frauds, Lord Young said: "Research shows conclusively that a high level of sweetener intake does no harm at all and may even do positive good. There is no evidence whatsoever that 'bribes', as they are technically known, do any damage whatsoever.

"Taken in small regular doses or even in one huge cheque, they encourage growth and keep everything flowing smoothly."

Lord Suit is £138 million.

Answers to Terrifically Boring '80s Quiz of the Decade

1. Mrs Thatcher.
2. Loadsamoney.
3. "We are a Grandmother."
4. Jeffrey Archer.
5. a) Ronald Reagan.
   b) Mrs Thatcher.
   c) Jeffrey Archer.
6. Perestroika.
7. Gang of Four.
8. a) Gotcha.
   b) The Gypsy Kings.
9. Margaret Thatcher, Margaret Drabble, Princess Margaret and Inspector Maigret.
0. Mel and Griff, scratch and sniff, Edwina Currie.

The picture shows Miss Erika Roe.

Earthquake — Thatcher to blame

by Our Disaster Staff
Sviatoslav Richter-Scales
and **San Andreas Whittam-Strobes**

Within seconds of half of San Francisco being demolished, the Labour Party's disaster spokesman John Prescott was calling for a major public enquiry into what he called "the disaster that was just waiting to happen".

Mr Prescott claimed that the ultimate responsibility for the disaster lay with Mrs Thatcher. "If she had not cut back across the board on safety procedures, seismological surveys and signalling equipment, this terrible tragedy could have been averted," he said.

California, Here She Comes

Meanwhile Mrs Thatcher cut short her visit to the Commonwealth conference in Malaya, in order "to see for herself" the extent of the California catastrophe.

Late last night Mrs Thatcher was reported to be touring hospitals in the San Francisco area, desperately searching for the bedside of a victim to be photographed beside.

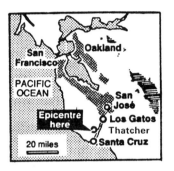

'How I whanged my donger in the Footlights'

Pt. 94 of Clive James's hilarious memoirs recalls his Cambridge career and is serialised by the *Observer* in the hope that it will persuade someone to buy it instead of the *Sunday Indie*. Now read on...

FOR a lad raised in a Melbourne suburb which had about as much culture as Sheena Easton's underwear Cambridge was a shock, I can tell you.

Imagine yours truly, twenty-four and full of the joys of the mind, sitting at the feet of F.R. Leavis, a man whose intellect spanned a great deal more than the Sydney Harbour Bridge on a wet Friday.

When he lectured on Lawrence to a packed Fitzwilliam Hall, zing went the strings of my heart.

And ping went the buttons on my flies when I found myself next to the gorgeous undergraduette, Germaine Randy, who later became the intellectual equivalent of a cross between the Crown Prince of Wittelsbach and Barry Humphries on speed with a wallaby in his trousers and a ton of rhino horn slipped into his billabong. It was actually Proust who said of Germaine that... *(That's enough James. Ed.)*

"Oh, Mr Gilbert . . . I'm afraid Mr Morton's out at the moment. He sends his regrets, however, and asks me to inform you that you're fired"

BRITAIN IN THE NINETIES

The Eye/Bori Survey

It's the cappuccino and fondue decade!

by Our Trend Staff
Peter Yorkie and **Adam Mars-Bar**

According to a poll of *Eye* readers, more than 79 per cent of people in Britain expect the '90s to offer them more cappuccino than ever before. Similarly, one in three Britons expect to eat fondue dishes in front of their TV.

The North/South divide is reflected in people's expectations of the availability of pistachio nuts. North of the Wash, a staggering 99 per cent have never heard of these delicious savoury appetisers. Yet in the affluent South, 100 per cent of people do not know what they are.

Complete rubbish

Four in five Englishmen expect to marry Spanish women during the next decade. But only one in seven Englishwomen are expected to have illegitimate children by Greek tourist representatives.

Overall, people in Britain are divided over the prospects for the country's future. A gloomy view is taken by 13 per cent, typified by one Deputy Prime Minister who referred to "litter-strewn draughty waiting rooms which are clearly the fault of this ghastly woman". But a more optimistic outlook is taken by one per cent of readers, including a typical commuter, Mr John Major.

"I think everything's wonderful," he said. "The trains run on time. There's no unemployment. And everyone earns £1,000 a week. It must be true. I just read it in the *Telegraph*."

That Kinnock Speech in full

KINNOCK: On my way to the conference hall this afternoon *(begins to giggle)* I was thinking that Maggie Thatcher *(corpses)* was rather like an Eskimo sitting in an igloo with a team of huskies *(audience begins to snigger)*. That's huskies, mind, not Russkies — although she's certainly got pretty fond of them all of a sudden. That's Maggie, right, with the Russians *(chokes on own joke)*. Anyway, this Eskimo, right, you'll like this bit, it's really great, Roy loved it, he nearly wet himself, or rather me because he was spitting all over the place, like he does on *Spitting Image*, or rather he doesn't, but the puppets do … and talking about puppets, what about Mrs Thatcher's Cabinet, they're not so much puppets as dummies *(doubles up and almost falls off stage with hysteria)*… anyway, here was this husky, which reminds me, I'm getting a bit husky myself, I think I'll have one of these Fishermen's Friends, which is more than Maggie's been, I mean a friend to the fishermen, in real terms their income has gone down by over 11 per cent in real terms, there's something pretty fishy about that, eh Maggie? *(Gets hiccups)* But seriously, back to the Eskimo, with the huskies, right, not the Russkies — I thought I'd recycle that one just to show how green we are, and talking of green, what about this Chris Patten? A bit like the same old pattern, if you ask me, the same old Tory pattern of death, decay, destruction and dehumanification that personifies the spirit of Thatcher's Britain. What was it the great poet Shelley said, and I think it could well be our inspiration for the Labour Government of the 90s, and make no mistake, we will be… not just the government of the 90s, but the custodians of the centuries to come *(audience applaud in hope of hearing punch line of joke about eskimo and huskies)*. I think it was in the poem *Ode To A Wild Welsh Windbag* that Shelley said:

> *"The ways of the world are passing strange*
> *Meet the challenge, make the change*
> *And generations not yet born*
> *Will live to see the Labour dawn."*

And no make no mistake, dawn it will be, if only we work together, unified and at one, in a totally unified way, to bring about whatever it is.

CHAIRMAN: Will you please get off Mr Kinnock. It's time for Arthur Scargill to lose us the next election.

"Looks like another cereal murder"

Millions flock to see dictator's palace

by Our Man in Oxford
Pergamon Wortshorne

Robert Maxwellescu – in happier days

Yesterday millions of sightseers queued round the clock in a remote part of the countryside to see for the first time the fabled palace of the world's most hated dictator, Robert Maxwellescu.

Many gasped openly at the astonishing display of wealth and vulgarity amassed by the publisher during his 40 years of tyranny over the Pergamon empire.

Said one amazed onlooker: "We had to queue in the *Mirror* canteen for our egg and chips while he was here having caviar ladled into his mouth on a silver spoon by Joe Haines."

Bob's Your Uncle Bulgaria

Crowds gaped as they saw the gigantic specially cast 60ft bath and the reinforced solid gold toilet seats made exclusively to fit "the Captain's" outsize frame. And then there were the fridges, each one of them crammed to bursting with huge pots of Albanian caviar and piles of Moscow gold.

The Captain's dressing room, the size of two tennis courts, contained 58 wardrobes, each one stuffed with vast silk pyjamas made from enough material to cover the M25.

Maxwell's private shoe collection, all hand made from pure crocodile skin, filled three floors of the place they are calling "Headington Hall".

Photographs in elaborate gilt frames of Maxwell's many children decorate the walls. Each of them was given a prominent posting in the Maxwell empire — Darren, Wayne, Enver, Todor, Kevin and little Jaruselski were all promoted, to the intense dismay of millions of ordinary workers and intellectuals (Pol Fot) whose backbreaking toil had sustained the dictator and his wife in their crazed dreams of world domination.

Robert Maxwell is 98.

ON OTHER PAGES

Queen Strips Maxwell of Peerage She Never Offered p.6

INTRODUCING VAZ, YOUR FAVOURITE COMIC!

10 things you didn't know about **Sir Anthony Nobody,** the man who dares to challenge Thatch, the Supreme Ruler of the Universe.

1. **Foreign sounding name, possibly German.**

2. **Foreign Office background, they're all poofs.**

3. **Favourite TV programme, Julian Clary's** *Sticky Moments.*

4. **Old Etonian, we know what they get up to.**

5. **Baronetcy, we know what the aristocracy are like.**

6. **With his dog, stick and grey hair, he looks like Michael Foot.**

7. **Appears to be happily married, often used as a front by homosexuals seeking high office.**

Traitor

8. **Silly educated voice.**

9. **War hero in World War Two — Count Tolstoy, please note!**

10. **Interests in** *Who's Who* **include "cooking" — need we say more?**

©The Sun, Mail, Express, etc, in cooperation with Central Office.

U2 NAPALM DEATH IRON MAIDEN

I QUITE LIKE RICHARD STILGOE

A Vet writes
Mad Cow Disease

As a vet, I am often asked these days: "How would you like a TV series?" But more of that later.

I am also asked as a vet about this terrifying new condition known as Mad Cow Disease (*Bovine spongiform enteritis*), which is sweeping through Britain and threatening the survival of all life as we know it.

What happens is that the old cow, or Mrs Thatcher (to give her her full medical name), starts foaming at the mouth and mooing in a strident, harsh, aggressive voice that can be heard for miles.

Sadly there is no cure for Mad Cow Disease, which is so virulent that unless the cow is forced to resign the whole nation becomes infected and dies.

NEXT WEEK: Mad Howe Disease (or Sleeping Sickness)

© A. Wet.

Red leaders lived in luxury as comrades starved

by **Dennis Potsdam**
Our Man On The Berlin Wall In The Dirty Mac

BEHIND locked gates up a 200-yard mud track in an East German forest lies the luxury bungalow hideaway of the former hated Party Chief, Egon Tözst.

Yesterday the people of East Germany reeled back in horror as TV cameras revealed for the first time the incredible life-style of the Red bosses who for years have lorded it over the masses behind Berlin's infamous Berlin Wall.

What the gasping East Germans goggled was a veritable Aladdin's Cave of Western-style luxury goods.

In Herr Tözst's five-room "palace", where he lived with his mother, Frau Ludmilla Tözst, he enjoyed such astonishing perks as:

● **a fridge**

● **an indoor lavatory**

● **a pre-war portable transistor radio in full working order.**

As the cameras roved round the hitherto hidden world where East Germany's Communist elite partyed the night away to forbidden Frankie Vaughan records smuggled in from the West, viewers saw Frau Tözst's shoe cupboard containing no less than three shoes, two of them matching.

Deutsche Marcos

"It is the Imelda Marcos Scandal writ large," said one shocked Leipzig hausfrau, as she gaped in disbelief at the seemingly endless supplies of potatoes which Herr Tözst had managed to hoard away under his Western-made bath.

Save the Whale Says Sir Jonah

𝕭𝖆𝖇𝖞𝖑𝖔𝖓 𝕿𝖎𝖒𝖊𝖘

2 shekels

BACKWARD WITH THE CHOSEN PEOPLE

BABEL PROJECT SAVED

*by Our City Staff **Solomon Rushdie***

THE multi-billion pound plan to build the world's largest tower has been saved after its worst-yet financial crisis. Yesterday bankers from every nation in the world pledged another 20 billion shekels to allow the next stage of the gigantic project to go ahead.

This, it is hoped, will allow the tower to be completed on schedule on 1st July 1993 BC.

Tunnel Vision

So far only the foundations of the giant structure have been half completed, at a cost to date of 718,000 billion shekels.

The contractors' initial estimate of the tower's cost was 35p.

Says the chairman of Ur-o-Tower, Mr Alistair Morecashplease: "We are now back on schedule to guarantee that the Tower will reach heaven by the target date."

Behind-the-scenes pressure from King Ozythatchias, who regards the tower as the supreme monument to her ten-year rule, is thought to have been responsible for the latest rescue package.

Still to be finalised, however, are the plans for "links" to the tower from all parts of Mesopotamia, which will involve the destruction of several hundred cities, including the Designated Areas of Outstanding Unnatural Vice at Sodom and Gomorrah.

That BBC shock Easter schedule in full

The BBC Religious Department is pleased to announce that this year the Festival of Easter will be marked by a series of "personal reflections" by six atheists on the sufferings of themselves at the hands of the media.

1. **Dr Marietta Higgs**, the Cleveland child expert, on the text: "Turn the other cheek; I've got this foolproof diagnosis."

2. **John Browne MP** on the text: "And a man shall put away his wife, and take her money."

3. **Ron Brown MP** on the text: "I win moral victory in knickers case."

4. **Ernest Saunders**, former chairman of Guinness, on the text: "And they robbed him and stripped him of all that he had."

5. **The Bishop of Durham** on the text: "O me of little faith."

6. **Larry Adler** on the text: "Did I ever tell you about the time I played with Duke Ellington, and he said 'Larry, you're the greatest, you're the tops'?"

(That's enough whingeing atheists — God.)

IN THE COURTS

Before Mr Justice Cocklecassock

600,000 red-bearded Cossacks filed into the High Court yesterday at the start of what has been billed as the "libel trial of the century".

In the dock is the upright figure of the legendary historian and novelist Count Tolstoy, who stands accused of writing an inflammatory pamphlet accusing the late Adolf Hitler of "war crimes".

Also involved in the case are the late Lord Stockton, Jack the Ripper and the ever-popular Mr Jeffrey Archer.

COCKLECASSOCK: Let us start with five minutes of attunement while we count our fees. Do I have any advice on how long this trial is likely to last?

SIR HARTLEY REDFACE *(counsel for Mr Robert Maxwell):* My Lord, we are hoping to string this one out for about three years. Is that convenient for all the parties?

SIR TITO GABOR QC *(counsel for the late King Zog of Albania):* Are we talking about cheques?

MR JUSTICE COCKLECASSOCK: No, it seems we are talking about Yugoslavs!

(Court erupts in huge gales of sycophantic laughter.)

MR JUSTICE COCKLECASSOCK: Or perhaps I should have said "Poles", referring of course to the so-called "Community Charge"!

(Court is cleared for several hours as barristers receive first-aid for injuries sustained by their hysterical laughter at this prime example of judicial wit)

MR JUSTICE COCKLECASSOCK: I would remind the Court that it is lunchtime. Perhaps we could get round to starting the case tomorrow afternoon?

(The Court then adjourned for 24 hours. On the resumption the following day, Lord Sun Alliance of Allalongtimeago, formerly Brigadier Toby Jugg, was called to the witness box)

SIR EPHRAIM: Would you like to talk for three hours about your distinguished war record and show us some slides?

LORD SUN: Indeed I would. It was the summer of '41 when things were at the blackest...

JUSTICE COCKLECASSOCK: As one of our most eminent war heroes and former leader of the Tory party, please feel free to sit down and speak inaudibly.

LORD SUN: Thank you my lord...
(Three hours later) ...My childhood was a happy one before the war clouds loomed.

SIR HARTLEY REDFACE: I put it to you, Mr Waldheim, that you are mistaken about certain events in the past.

LORD SUN *(to Judge):* My Lord, I am not accustomed to being accused of telling lies by some jumped up Johnny in a wig.

COCKLECASSOCK: I fully understand your distress, My Lord. Just think of Sir Ephraim as a soldier doing his duty.

LORD SUN: Shoot him!

COCKLECASSOCK: Would that it were within the prerogative of this court to execute people in the manner to which you are no doubt accustomed.

SIR RAMPTON BATMAN *(for Count Nikolai Tallstory):* My Lord, I would like to call the following: The Grand Duke Ferdinand of Marcos, the late General Von Straubenzee, leader of the Imperial War Dragons, Dr Christopher Barkworth and of course Joanna Lumley.

COCKLECASSOCK: Who is Joanna Lumley?

(Laughter)

COCKLECASSOCK: This is not a variety show. We are discussing a serious issue of grave importance. That is to say whether or no Mr Robert Maxwell, the distinguished war hero and philanthropist was responsible for handing over thousands of East German refugees to be tortured by Herr Honeker's secret police.

(The case continues)

"He keeps dancing with me"

IN THE COURTS

The case of the 600,000 Red-Bearded Cossacks (continued).

940th year.

(Mr Justice Cocklecassock continues his summing-up)

MR JUSTICE COCKLE-CASSOCK: We now turn to the evidence put forward by the prisoner, Count Tallstory, or rather the lack of evidence, one might say — but that, members of the jury, is for you to decide.

You will remember the letter he sent to his fellow conspirator, as you may think, Mr Nigel Nutts — "We've got the old war criminal by the short and curlies." Now, what you have to consider is this: were those the words of a responsible historian, carefully weighing the evidence, or the drink-induced rantings of a crazed lunatic with a foreign name? It is not, of course, for me to decide that the latter description comes nearer to the facts of the case, though of course it does. Again, that is entirely a matter for you, and you alone, to decide.

We then turn to the evidence given by Captain Tweed, whom you remember as the gentleman with the high-pitched voice who told us how he had "sobbed his heart out" over the fate of the Cossacks. What a pathetic nancy-boy, you may have thought, members of the jury. Or, on the contrary, you may have thought that Captain Tweed was a conscientious and caring officer who was only doing his duty. Again, this is a matter for you and you alone — to make up your minds whether he was or was not a whingeing crybaby and bedwetter, of the type that nearly lost us the war.

There is not time for me to go in detail into the evidence given to the court by the 600,000 Cossacks and Yugoslavs. They, members of the jury, were the foreign gentlemen whom we all found it rather difficult to understand, and impossible to believe — though believe them you may. That is your privilege, though I would advise against it.

Having dismissed from our minds the evidence produced on behalf of Count Tallstory, let us now look carefully at his co-defendant, Mr Nutter. He tells us a sorry cock and bull story about some insurance policy, which is of course quite irrelevant to the matters before this court. Had these gallant warriors from the Steppes, however, had the forethought to insure themselves with the Sun Alliance Insurance Company against accidental massacre by Lord Allalongtimeago, then you might think there would have been a rather happier ending to the story!

(Cocklecassock looks amused at his attempted joke and waits for press to copy it down as an example of judicial wit)

COCKLECASSOCK: As far as I can see, Mr Nutts first became unhinged by his ridiculous vendetta against Lord Allalongtimeago. He was then completely taken in by the farrago of nonsense published by Count Tallstory in his book, *I Name Britain's Secret 50,000 War Criminals…*

MR NIGEL NUTTS: I must protest. This is a total travesty of the truth. You obviously haven't been listening to the evidence, you old git…

(Jury wakes up, showing first signs of interest for several months)

NUTTS: You call this justice? You're a disgrace to your profession. I have never met Count Tallstory in my life. I have nothing to do with all this. I am totally innocent of all charges. I am going to repatriate myself to a desert island before I am massacred by the entire British establishment, led by such notorious war criminals as Lord Allalongtimeago, Sir Winston Churchill and you yourself, My Lord. I warn you, you would be hearing from my solicitors, if I had any.

(Nutts storms out of court to standing ovation from public gallery)

MR JUSTICE COCKITALLUP: I would ask the jury to strike from their minds this most distressing scene which we have just witnessed. I would in particular ask that it should not prejudice in any way the jury's conclusion that Mr Nutts is obviously of unsound mind and is probably missing as many screws in the top storey as his partner in crime, the self-styled historian and liar Count Tallstory. You may think, on the other hand, something else. That is entirely a matter for me to decide.

SIR RAMPTON BATMAN QC: With the greatest possible respect, My Lord, are you not possibly going a little, as we lawyers say, OTT yourself in this matter?

MR JUSTICE CUCKOO-CARROT: I would ask the Court Usher, Mrs Dalrymple, to strike Sir Rampton about the head with her mop until dead. It is clearly the only language he understands.

Now, where was I? Oh yes. Lord Allalongtimeago, as you may long since have decided, members of the jury, was one of the most distinguished war heroes of his day — although there has been some lengthy debate as to precisely what day that was!

(Sycophantic laughter from Sir Rampton, who is attempting to fight off the advancing Mrs Dalrymple by peeling £50 notes from a thick wad and waving them at the grim-faced cleaning lady)

MR JUSTICE COCKLE-CARVEUP: Lord Allalongtimeago is also a peer of the realm, a former chairman of one of our most respected public companies, and completely innocent of all charges brought against him.

On the other hand, members of the jury, you may consider that Lord Allalongtimeago is a gentleman, a good husband, a devoted father, and precisely the sort of chap one could spend an agreeable evening with at the club.

That, ladies and gentlemen of the jury, is what you have to decide. It is entirely up to you.

When it comes to the amount of damages that you should award against Count Tallstory for this unparalleled outrage — should you so deem it — you are not to think in terms of Donald Duck…

(Final desperate sycophantic laughter from losing barrister)

COCKLECASSOCK: …That is to say, the type of sum which, were it to be invested, would yield an increment of, let us say, the value of an agreeable house in the Cotswolds. That would be inappropriate, and might lead to unfortunate consequences, such as the Court of Appeal deciding that I've cocked up the summing-up, should they so think.

And now I must ask you to retire to consider my verdict.

"Sorry, we don't serve food"

DAVE RUDD.

Major's Budget — how it affects you

Married working woman, with four grown-up children. Husband in part-time employment. Current income: **£5,438 million.** *Under the provisions of the Budget she will be £22 million better off.*

Widow-pensioner living alone in West End of London and Scottish castle. Spirit drinker. Current income: **£439,000.** *After the Budget: £32,412 better off.*

Single parent, two children of school age, many horses, living in Gloucestershire. Does part-time voluntary work. Current income: **£2,816,000.** *After Budget: £977,000 better off.*

Divorced woman, living alone, heavy smoker and drinker. Current income: **£212,462.** *After Budget: £52,600 better off.*

Single man in early 20s, with low-paid job in tea industry. Current income: **27p.** *After Budget: no change.*

Kray Twins buy Harrods

by Our City Staff
Ivan the Fallible

In a move that has delighted the City, the controversial Kray brothers were yesterday given the green light by Trade Secretary Nicholas Ridley to buy the world-famous department store Harrods.

"My department has received assurances that Mr Ronald and Mr Reginald Kray are businessmen of the highest repute, descended from well-known East End families, who have over the years built up a considerable fortune in antique silver, gold bullion, video recorders and voluntary contributions from many branches of the entertainment industry," Mr Ridley told the House.

"I am further assured by their solicitors, Messrs Rubinstein, Cosh, that their clients had English nannies and had been educated at the finest schools in Bethnal Green," Mr Ridley said.

You're Fayed

Another testimonial to the "unimpeachable financial integrity" of the Kray brothers was provided by the merchant bankers Kleinworts and All, who said that they were confident that "every penny the Krays possess is from their own hard-earned savings".

Mr Norman Tebbit immediately welcomed the proposed purchase of Harrods by, as he put it, "two *bona fide* Englishmen who represent all that is best in the enterprise culture of the late 'sixties".

However, Mr Charles "Tiny" Richardson, leader of a rival "group" of financiers based in South London who also wished to purchase the store, said last night: "We was robbed. It is nothing less than an outrage. The government must step in."

Lord Young is 63.

After 30 years as Britain's youngest editor of the Spectator ("The best-written weekly periodical in English" — G. Greene, 1931), Charles Moore has decided it is time to move on to pastures new. He has told friends that he is going to spend the next six months in the country "writing a novel". Now read on . . .

Old at Heart
Charles Moore

The story of one man's passionate love for the Old Prayer Book

CRISPIN looked out of his window onto the all-too-familiar Bloomsbury street scene. How many times, he thought, had he gazed out of that window, watching the elderly figure of traffic warden P149 pinning a ticket to some ghastly Volvo? How tiresome it had all become, this job of being editor of the *Discriminator.*

Was it only six years ago that he had taken over the editor's chair from the legendary figure of Alexander Treasurer? Then, at the age of 19, the world had seemed at his feet. Cabinet Ministers at the famous weekly *Discriminator* lunches. Invitations to appear on the BBC's *Question Night*. Columns in the *Daily Excess*. The world had seemed at his feet, a veritable oyster to be savoured like a vintage wine or a rich Havana cigar.

But for months now a dreadful feeling of ennui had been creeping upon him. He gazed with distaste at the congealed cup of coffee that had been placed on his desk an hour before by Miss Patterson.

How many more times would he have to ring up his columnist Jeff O'Toole on Wednesday mornings to find out yet again why his copy was terrible? *(Don't you mean 'late'? Ed.)* How many more times would he have to rack his brains for a diary paragraph about these awful new electronic ticket machines on the underground — or the unsightly "bar codes" which now, by law, had to disfigure the front cover of the *Discriminator*?

A shudder of distaste for everything about this horrible, plastic, throwaway, electronic modern world ran through his dark-suited frame.

He would have to throw it all in and write a novel. But what could he, Crispin Dale, possibly write about?

Then, suddenly, it came to him. A character called Clovis Hill would be his hero. Clovis Hill, the Old Etonian editor of a fashionable magazine called *"The Inquisitor"*.

He could see how it would begin.

"It was a dark and stormy night and Clovis looked out of his window…" *(Continued p. 94)*

When democracy spells dictatorship

by Professor Norman Brainstone

Professor Brainstone, Cobb Professor of Emotional Studies at Tired College, Oxford, has recently returned from a two day visit to Russia. His recent publications include 17 "Why Oh Why?" pieces in the Daily Mail.

MAKE no mistake, Gorbachev may look like a reformer but beneath his reasonable exterior he is a hardline Marxist-Leninist through and through.

All of his so-called "liberalisations" have merely been part of a sinister masterplan as fiendishly cunning as anything that Lenin himself might have devised.

The break up of the Warsaw Pact may seem like the end of an era

but, studied more closely (through this battle of Glasnost Vodka which I obtained at the Leningrad Duty Free), it is simply Gorbachev's method of imposing supreme communist power over countries like Hungary, Poland and East Germany.

And take the internal developments being so widely hailed as a breakthrough. What else can multi-party parliamentary democracy mean except a return to stalinist terror on a huge scale?

Karl Marx foresaw how it would be. A bourgeois parliament will inevitably fragment into bickering cliques (as in Dusseldorf in 1926) leaving the way clear for the strong man to emerge — in this case Generalissimo Gorbachev.

As a historian, I can see it all. And, I tell you, don't trust the Reds. Vote Conservative.

TOMORROW: Professor Brainstone visits Rumania and predicts the rise of a new Tito to restore order.

NEXT CUSTOMER

BUCHAREST TIMES

2½ Lei

MOBS STORM THATCHESCU STRONGHOLDS

from the Romanian News Agency, Taff

Cities all over Britain were brought to a halt yesterday as angry mobs went on the rampage in protest against the hated Thatchescu regime.

Unrest has been boiling up for weeks, as the British people have groaned under an ever-growing yoke of runaway inflation, soaring interest rates and, above all, the hated "poll tax", which is universally regarded as yet another symptom of the ever-growing megalomania of the "Supreme Ruler of the Universe", as Mme Thatchescu insists on being called.

Megaloromania

Observers noted that the latest wave of mass demonstrations has spread chaos into such traditional Party homelands as Iron-Maidenhead, Nagorno-Tunbridge Wells and Sunday-Timisoara.

However, Party chief Kenneth Bakescu, head of the hated Securitori, dismissed the protestors as "just a tiny minority of paid agitators brought in from outside in order to divert attention from the heroic progress being made on the most lasting monument to the glorious achievement of the Thatchescu regime, the Channel Tunnel."

Paid agitators stir up violence

Modern History

Core Curriculum Pt 94.

The dates children must know

1911:
Margaret Hilda Thatcher born.

1979:
Margaret Thatcher becomes Leader of the Conservative Party.

1980:
Edward Heath condemned to death.

1982:
The Battle of the Falklands. Victory for British forces under Mrs Thatcher.

1983:
The Battle of Scargill. Mrs Thatcher defeats Baron Scargill.

1984:
The Battle of Wapping. Mrs Thatcher and her general Prince Rupert of Murdoch defeat rebel

Queen Brenda and her hordes of print workers.

1984:
Mrs Thatcher re-elected with 90 per cent of poll.

1988:
Mrs Thatcher re-elected with 99 per cent of poll.

1990:
The Poll-Taxer's Revolt. Mrs Thatcher crushes anarchist insurrection.

1991:
Execution of Michael Heseltine.

1992:
Mrs Thatcher re-elected with 100 per cent of poll.

(That's enough dates — Ed)

  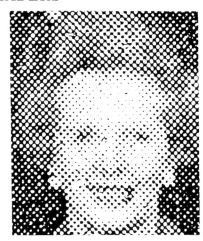

DO YOU KNOW THESE PEOPLE?

by Our Political Staff **John Coletax**

Police last night issued photographs, cut out of the *Daily Telegraph*, of people whom they wish to interview in connection with the recent Poll Tax disturbances all over England. Inspector Knacker of the Yard has asked for members of the public who may know the so-called "Whitehall Three" to come forward with any information that could lead to the arrest of the trio believed to be behind the shocking outbreaks of mass violence.

1. "Brylcreem Ken". He is believed to be in his mid-50s, with long greasy hair, glasses and a smirking expression. Highly politically motivated, "Ken" belongs to a tiny group of fanatics known as the "Suck Up To Thatch Tendency".

2. Unknown man in blue. This suspect was definitely identified in the Trafalgar Square area on the day of the riots. He was wearing a policeman's helmet and lashing out at passers-by with a long stick, while they went about their Christmas shopping.

3. "Grantham Maggie". A teenage runaway who came to the bright lights of London in search of total power. Says her sister: "We still love her, even if no one else does. Whatever she may have done, she is still family."

Those targets in full

In the ongoing war against the ruling establishment, there are ~~inevitab~~ ~~innevit~~ always casualties. However they are a necessary ~~addjunk~~ part of the bringing down of the upper class ~~oligaga~~ system. That is why the following targets were singled out by our warriors in last Saturday's heroic battle against the oppressors.

1. "Casa Fratelli", Italian Cheese, Charlotte Street. Purveyor of Italian comestibles, owned by Fratelli family.

2. "Nick-Nax — Last-Minute Birthday Gifts a Speciality", Goodge Street. Purveyor of Snoopy posters and Garfield badges. Owned by Mrs Smallpiece.

3. The Apollo Kebab House, Rathbone Place. Purveyor of Turkish late-night cuisine. Owned by brothers Donner and Sheesh Kubab.

4. "Hang On A Minute!" Purveyors of photographic development services. Also Fax Bureau and Colour Photocopying. Owned by Mr Perkins (90).

5. Patel's Newsagent and Tobacconist, Tottenham Street. Fine-quality magazines and cough sweets by the till. Owned by Eddie Patel.

"I'm playing the Maradona way!"

School news

St. Cake's

Strangeways Term opened today. There are 413 boys in the school (and three on the roof). M.V.P. Catalytic-Converter (Greens) is Senior Porritt. Miss C.F.C. Global-Warming (Ozones) is Junior Conservator. Mr H.G.V. Rates has left the school and has been replaced by Mr N.B.G. Polltax as Chairman of the St. Cake's 1990 Appeal Fund. We regret to announce the death of Simon Wormwood-Scrubs (Portillos), which leaves only two boys remaining on the roof. Mandela Day (formerly Founder's Day) will be taken on 24 June. The preacher will be the Rev. Jesse Jackson (OC?). There will be six performances of *Shir-ley Valentine* in the Kenneth Branagh Theatre Space from 20 June. Tickets from the Bursar, Maj. S. Hussein, "Noriega", Cakes Road. The annual Old Cakeians v. St. Biscuit's cricket match will be played on Fergie's Bottom on 1 July. We regret to announce the death of Crispin Holloway (Mellors), which leaves only one boy on the roof. Quittings will be on 8 July, except in the case of Adam Risley (Waddingtons), who is still refusing to come down from the roof and is really letting down the school and his parents rather badly. We regret to announce that the North Wing is now on fire. Will all boys please assemble in an orderly fashion on the Parade Ground. The annual Dinner and Dance has had to be postponed.

Wee Willie Whingie

(Continuing the serialisation of the memoirs of Mr David Steel, formerly leader of the Liberal Party)

I always had the greatest admiration for my predecessor Jeremy Thorpe. He was a man of great gifts who brought the Liberal Party a wealth of experience, dedication and talent.

Unfortunately there was a darker side to Jeremy which was to bring our once great party into disrepute. Even when I took over, he refused to shut up and go away. He insisted on remaining an MP and consistently undermined me by appearing at the party conference with his silly suits and watchchain.

If it had not been for this depraved lunatic, I would have been swept to power on a tide of Liberal support years ago.

I still retain great affection for Jeremy and wish him well in his retirement.

Another man I wish well in retirement is David Owen. He is a man of enormous abilities, with extraordinary vision, courage and leadership potential.

Our Alliance was the most important political movement this century. If it had not been for his pigheadedness and arrogance I would have been swept to power in 1983 on a tide of third party enthusiasm.

Nevertheless, I still retain great affection for David Owen and it gives me no pleasure at all to point out that he is entirely washed up and has become an object of derision and pity.

NEXT WEEK: How Callaghan offered me the Prime Ministership and Spitting Image ruined it for me.

INTRODUCING VIV, YOUR FAVOURITE COMIC

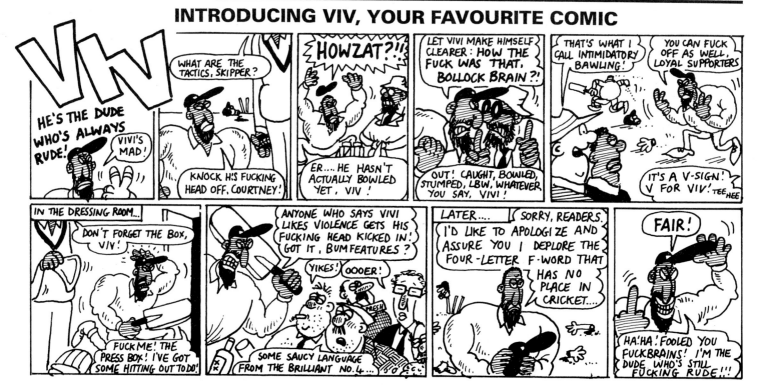

Your Cut Out 'n' Keep Guide To What's On Radio Five

9:00 News and weather.

9:05 World service.

11:00 This week's composer, Kalashnikov *(see Radio 3)*.

12:00 *Hey there groovy young people!* With DJ's Mike Hasbeen and Dave Oldie.

1:00 News and weather.

2:00 For schools. Julian Clary talks to sixteen year olds about vital issues of the day. This week: Masturbation.

2:05 Phone-in with complaints about the previous programme with Emma Fraud and Angela Runoff.

3:00 World service. Rural life in Namibia. *(Repeat from 1968).*

4:00 For the Under-3's. Sammy Spider goes to the Notting Hill Carnival.

5:00 *Hi kids, listen in to this!* With Simon Fanclub.

7:00 *Euro-Beat.* Listeners phone in from Luxembourg with their requests.

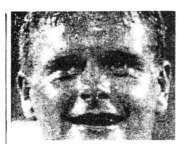

It's him again

8:00 *Wow! Crucial!* A new soap opera for 11-14 year olds set in a youth club in Neasden.

9:00 *Iphigenia in Paxo* by Desmond Stoddy and the Radiophonic Workshop. *(See Radio 3).*

11:00 "Hey! Why are you still awake?" with Frank Bruno, "Gazza" Gascoigne and "Mazza" Montgomery-Massingberd. *(Shurely shome mishtake?)*

12:00 Closedown. *(Probably for good)*

Do you like Simple Minds?

Well, I've always supported you... Whoops, bit political... Yes, indeed... etc.

WEMBLEY 1990

The Mandela Concert

SIR — No doubt many of your readers who, like me, sat through five hours of caterwauling jungle music on Easter Monday will have been sickened, nauseated and disgusted by the spectacle of Her Majesty's Leader of the Opposition giving the Nazi salute to a convicted mass-murderer, with a so-called Christian bishop at his side. I did not fight in two world wars to see the British Broadcasting Corporation squandering my hard-earned licence fee on such blatant Communist propaganda which in the newly-liberated nations of Eastern Europe would be laughed to scorn.

Yours faithfully,
SIR BUFTON TUFTON
The Old Rectory, Barkworth, Somerset.

SIR — No one could abhor apartheid more than I. Yet the sight of this African ex-convict being invited to this country by the BBC, to stand up in front of millions of dope-crazed anarchists to criticise the democratically elected leader of our country, frankly sickened, disgusted and nauseated me. How dare this tinpot African dictator tell Mrs Thatcher how to run his country with, I may say, the full endorsement of our own home-grown Marxists in the C of E and the Labour Party. I say Mr Marmaduke Hussey should resign immediately.

Yours faithfully,
SIR HERBERT GUSSET
Moorhens-on-the-Brain, Bristol.

SIR — Those of us who were privileged to be at Wembley last Monday will never forget the feeling of utter transcendental peace and joy which attended that moment when at last in the flesh we saw Him. At that moment inevitably many of us will have reflected how for 27 years He lay in darkness, crucified on the cross of apartheid. But then, thanks to the BBC, we saw the stone rolled away, and there He stood revealed in all His Glory. We read in the Bible of the feeding of the five thousand. But the BBC has in a very real sense fed the billion! Thank you, St Marmalade, my £91 has been well spent.

Yours in Mandala,
REV. J.C. FLANNEL
Chair, All-Faith Team
Outreach Project, Toxteth.

SIR — Did I read that some of your readers are mentioning the name Mandela? If so, may I be the first to associate my name with his?

Yours very sincerely indeed,
REV. JESSE JACKSON
The Next President of the United States,
c/o The Free Winston Silcott Campaign, Blakelock, Staffs.

"Harry Secombe, Harry Secombe, Secombe Secombe, Harry Harry . . ."

"He's a Vietnam vet"

LETTERS TO THE EDITOR

From Mr Nigel West MP (better known as world-famous spy expert Chapman Pincher).

Sir — Although I have no personal knowledge of the late Mr Farzad Bazoft, it is quite clear to me as a world-famous spy expert that Mr Bazoft was just the sort of person who would have been recruited as an Agent by Mossad, the notorious Iranian secret service. Although I have no evidence for this, I am convinced that Mr Bazoft was probably engaged in a special undercover mission to kill the Ayatollah Khomeini, thus dragging the world into World War III, thereby incidentally discrediting the *Observer* which, as is well known, has been a favoured recruiting ground for the CIA since the days of the notorious Fifth Man, Sir Anthony Blunt.
Yours faithfully,
RUPERT ALLAH'S-SON,
Little Tory, Berks.

From the Chairman of the Anglo-Iraq Chamber of Commerce, Sir William Greed.

Sir — Whilst utterly deploring the barbaric execution of an innocent journalist, I feel however that we should not allow our very natural revulsion at this tragic event to stand in the way of our desire to make large amounts of money from the Iraqis. Your readers may be interested to know that my own company, Greed Chemical Warfare Technology plc, managed in the teeth of the fiercest foreign competition from South Africa, Chile and North Korea, to land contracts with the Iraqi government worth £1.2 million for Great Britain for supplying the agricultural fertiliser "Kurdo-cide" for use in the infertile northern parts of the country.

This contract is only a small example of what this country could throw away, if we allow the hysteria over the judicial execution of a proven spy, bank robber and journalist to deflect us from the true purpose of promoting Anglo-Iraqi friendship.
Yours faithfully,
SIR WILLIAM GREED,
Greed CWT plc,
Porton Down, Wilts.

From Sir Norman Rottweiler MP, Chairman of the Anglo-Iraqi Inter-Parliamentary Union.

Sir — Whilst utterly deploring the barbaric murder of an investigative spy, I feel that we should not allow our natural revulsion at his irresponsible undercover work for Mossad to blind us to the overriding necessity of executing him under well-established Islamic legal proceedings. On a recent visit to Baghdad, with 24 of my parliamentary colleagues of all parties, we were privileged to be granted a 10-minute audience with President Saddam Insein. We were all struck by his immense warmth and humanity, as well as his concern for all of his people. It is unthinkable that such a saintly figure would allow any act of injustice to take place anywhere in his country, which deserves the wholehearted support of everyone of goodwill in Great Britain.
Yours faithfully,
SIR NORMAN ROTTWEILER,
Great Backhander, Hants.

The Bazoft Dilemma

The tragic affair of Mr Farzad Bazoft is arguably the gravest breach of human rights by a sovereign state since the end of the Second World War. President Insein of Iraq has placed himself firmly beyond the pale with his barbaric disregard for even the most basic standards of civilised conduct.

It would, however, be a mistake to over-react to this unforgivable atrocity by calling for precipitate international measures designed to put pressure on the Iraqi government or its leader. Experience has all too often shown that hasty and ill-considered retaliatory actions of this type can be at best counter-productive and at worst catastrophic... President Carter... Rhodesian sanctions... best to do nothing.

Furthermore, it is no good trying to disguise the fact that Mr Bazoft was scarcely the stuff of which true martyrs are made. Not only was he a man with a criminal record, but he also worked for a rival paper, the *Observer*... Mr Donald Trelford... Pamella Bordes... nightclubs... Worsthorne was right... very shady business indeed.

In conclusion, it must be said that there are many questions about Mr Bazoft's sinister and reckless mission which have remained unanswered... obviously a spy... foreigner... got what was coming to him... that little creep Trelford.
© *All newspapers apart from the Observer.*

"Let me introduce my other half"

Glenda on Glenda

At 55, Glenda Slagson is to stand as Labour candidate for Neasden North. Glenda Slagg talked to her.

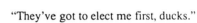

Pictures: Gavin Jurke.

"ANOTHER sugar in your tea, love?" The voice is unmistakable as she plonks a chipped mug down on the floor of her Victorian kitchen. We both sit cross-legged in a room that is spartan, efficient and yet feminine and warm. It exactly reflects the actress herself (*I thought it might — Ed.*) as she tells me about Labour's policies for urban renewal in the inner cities.

I look at the face, older now with grey hairs streaking the flaming gold — a face we all remember from *The Music Lovers*, (*fill in sub*), and so many more.

But now it is plain, scrubbed, sans make-up, exactly reflecting the actress herself (*We get the idea — Ed.*).

"Honestly, love," she declaims as she stands in the bay window and stares out across the overgrown garden. "That's what people need. I've never been afraid to speak my mind. I'm a northern lass at heart."

We laugh and I decide to be blunt in return (*I bet you weren't — Ed.*). How would she cope with exchanging international megastardom in such films as *The Music Lovers* and (*fill in again, sub*) for the humdrum obscurity of the Labour back benches?

"They've got to elect me first, ducks."

We laugh, and she strokes a stray cat that has climbed onto the window sill.

"There are too many homeless folk nowadays, what with this poll tax and everything... caring... sharing... Neil Kinnock... hardest role of my life... all the world's a stage... was that alright, love? Oh dear, I've dried... Vote Labour..."

I leave her reflecting that the media have hyped the whole thing up absurdly — she is, after all, just another Labour candidate.

I sympathise as my photographer sets up for an afternoon's shoot, and I ring the editor to hold at least three pages (*Make it four — Ed.*).

NEXT WEEK: Glenda on Seb. This candidate will run and run.

Queen visits St Cake's

by Our Man at St Cake's
Hugh Montgomery-Massivesnob O.C.

Her Majesty the Queen delighted hundreds of Old Boys and parents yesterday when she arrived by helicopter on the hallowed turf of the Lower Upper to award the boys of St Cake's school a special "halfer" (whole day's holiday) in honour of the school's 75th anniversary.

There were three "huzzahs" for Her Majesty, led by the Head Muppet J.M.D. Merchant-Banker (Yeltsin's), as the school choristers launched into the familiar verses of the school song:

*When our locks are old and
                    hoary
Our thoughts will turn to
                    former glory
When we stood with willow
                    raised in hand
Knowing that St Cake's was
        the best school in the land.*

(To the tune of *Men of Harlech* by Andrew Lloyd-Webber O.C.)

Earlier, in the St Kipling's School Chapel, the Archbishop of York, The Most Rev John Nogood, had preached a sermon on the text "Ye cannot serve both God and Mammon, but an Old Cakeian can have a good try".

"Nowadays, in a very real sense," said the Archbishop, "when he goes out into the world, the Old Cakeian can no longer expect automatically to become Prime Minister or Viceroy of India. He is more likely to spend his days gazing into an VDU somewhere in the City of London, calculating how much money he has made since the markets opened that morning. But this in its way is just as noble a calling as the army, the civil service or the television."

Following her reception, the Queen was taken on a tour of the new Safeway Language Lab complex, where she saw hundreds of eager young Cakeians being made familiar with the languages they will need when they enter the Common Market Oldboy Network in 1992.

"How long have you been here?" joked the Duke of Edinburgh to "new bod" P.D.Q. Burchill, son of the distinguished novelist and playwright Dame Judy Burchill.

Before leaving, the Queen was conducted to the Wilbursmith Library, where she was addressed in Latin by the Senior Gobbet, N.R.S. Dellingpole (Hasting's), who expressed the wish that in 75 years' time the Queen or her successor might once again "graciously descend from the heavens in her celestial device" ("ex coelo descenderit in helicoptero Budgio plagiarensis").

St Cakes is 75.

ON OTHER PAGES

THE BOOK OF SHAMIR

Chapter 94: The Promised Land

1. And there were dwelling in the land of Russ-i-a certain Jews, who were sore afflicted, for their hearts were heavy.

2. And they longed to journey to the promised land, which is flowing with milk and honey.

3. Then came a new ruler in the land of Russ-i-a, that was called Gor-bo. And they knew him by the mark upon his head, and they said: "Behold, here is a sign from the Lord that this shall be he who releaseth us from bondage."

4. And so it came to pass that Gor-bo said unto the children of Israel that lived in Russ-i-a: "Verily I say unto you that you can depart in peace and go out of our land, even the land of Glas-nost and Peres-troika, which is to say 'yea, we have no potatoes'."

5. Then the children of Israel rejoiced exceedingly and said with one voice: "Blessed is Gor-bo. For now we can gird up our loins and go even unto the Promised Land, which is to say the land of Man-hat-tan and the island that is called Long.

6. "And there we shall have all that our hearts desire. We shall dwell in the condom-iniums on the Eastern side, which is lower, and eat of the fruit of the cream cheese bagel and hearken unto the sayings of the prophet Jack-ie Mas-on, on the way that is broad."

7. And the children of Israel could not believe their luck, already.

8. And they gathered up their belongings and all that was theirs and prepared for the journey to the promised land.

9. And lo they journeyed even from She-rem-et-yevo and they came by night even unto the ending of their journey.

10. And, behold, when they arrived, Shamir came forth to greet them, saying: "O, ye children of Israel, ye are thrice welcome into the land of your forefathers."

11. And they shook their heads and said among themselves: "What is Shamir doing in New York? Verily, there must be some mistake."

12. But Shamir rebuked them, saying: "O, ye of little money, dost thou think that thou wilt dwell in the land of the Deli-cat-essenes?

13. "For, lo, it is written, by the sweat of your brow shall ye dwell in the desert, and ye shall there pitch your tents and multiply an hundredfold, until ye shall be numbered even as the children of the sons of Thom who swarm upon the sands of Eilat from January to March *(midwinter break, special offer)*, drinking the juice of the pinacolada tree."

14. Then Shamir leadeth them into the wilderness that is called the West Bank, and they came at last unto a village.

15. And Shamir said unto them: "Lo, the bus terminateth here. Here is the land that is promised to you, where ye shall dwell, even unto the ending of your days."

16. And the children of Israel that were from the land of Russ-i-a looked around them and said unto Shamir: "How can it be that we should settle in this place? For behold, on every side, it appeareth that there already dwell here a multitude of Arab-ites, Araf-ites, Shi-ites and sons of Yasser, which is to say he who weareth the towel upon his head.

17. "How can this be the promised land? For these territories, as their name implieth, are already occupied."

18. And Shamir laughed them to scorn, saying unto them: "There is no problem. Go forth in peace and smite the Arab-ites and the Araf-ites, and lay waste their dwellings, and, behold, the land shall soon be thine, even as it hath been promised."

ALABAMA WELCOMES CAREFUL DRIVERS HAVE A NICE DAY.

MIKE TURNER.

ROADWORKS NEXT 2 MILES

NEW HIGGINS SENSATION

by **Donald Trelford**, Our Man At The Crucible With The Can Of Low-Alcohol Full-Strengh Export Headbanger Lager And The Packet Of Extra-Slim Julietta Bravo Cigars.

THE WORLD of snooker was rocked to its foundations last night when the crowded auditorium of the Sheffield Crucible witnessed amazing scenes involving snooker's "bad boy", Mr Alex "Hurricocaine" Higgins.

Halfway through the first frame, spectators and TV viewers gasped as the veteran Northern Ireland ace and former world champion bent down over the table and deliberately hit a ball.

Said one close observer: "I couldn't believe my eyes. Alex had been behaving quite normally up until then, missing everything and uttering obscenities, when suddenly he blatantly and without provocation bashed this poor red ball right into the pocket."

Long Rest

Officials last night refused to comment on Higgins's outrageous behaviour. Said a spokesman for BOWTIE (snooker's governing body): "We will have to see a video replay of the alleged incident before doing nothing. Mr Higgins knows the score. It's 10-0."

However, last night Higgins was unrepentant.

"I am what I am. People pay to see me smacking the balls about a bit. They would soon get bored if all I did was to go round headbutting officials and issuing death threats to my opponents."

Ted Lowe is 108.

The Alternative Rocky Horror Service Book

No. 94: The Ordination of an Advertising Agency to represent the Church of England.

The President: Who is it who shall run this idea up the flagpole and see who saluteth it?

The Agents: We are N____ and M____ (or it may be D, B, B, and D or C, L, P, R, J, K, Da Souza).

THE HOLY COMMUNICATION

The President: Dearly beloved, we are gathered here in a meeting and do not wish to be disturbed by the switchboard.

All: Let's have lunch.

President: If anyone here has a window free let them speak now.

(The Agents shall then consult their filofaxes or it may be Le Fax or another such leatherbound personalised ringbinder)

The Agents: We're looking at the end of September.

The President: Let us pencil it in.

All: We will ring to confirm.

THE PRESENTATION

The President: So how do you see this one, basically?

The Agents: The creative department have roughed out a few ideas.

The President: Bring them forth that we may praise them.

All: Great. Terrific. Magic.

THE READING

(The Account Directors or some such officials shall then read the slogans)

1st Director: Does you does or does you don't take communion regularly?

2nd Director: He is. Are you?

3rd Director: I'm with the Bishop of Woolwich.

4th Director: Naughty but Nicean Creed.

All: Is that all you have?

5th Director: Happiness is a hamlet with a beautiful church in it.

6th Director: We haven't quite finished this one but we're hoping to get Mel and Griff to do it.

All: What about Fry and Laurie?

President: Maybe Harold Enfield is free?

(At this point the congregation shall all look at their watches and then ring their secretaries N____ and M____ or it may be Sophie, Venetia, Charlotte and Sarah)

All: Are there any messages?

Secretaries: Your wife rang about the car.

THE BLESSING

The President: I now declare you to be our agency. Go forth and pitch.

The Agents: Thank God for that.

THE OFFERTORY

(At this point huge sums of money shall be collected from the church and given to the advertising agents. During this a suitable piece of music shall be played, such as "Take My Breath Away" or the theme tune from the Yellow Pages ad where old Ted gets a new motor mower)

THE DISMISSAL

The President: This stuff's terrible. You're fired.

(The congregation shall then adjourn to Kettner's to tell their secretaries what a terrible day they've had)

OBITUARIES

Laurence Vole

LAURENCE VOLE was for many years a well-known figure in Fitzrovia, where his distinctive lifestyle won him many admirers.

Vole was educated at Marylebone Grammar School, although he left at the age of 16 to travel in Belgium. In later years he would often reminisce about his youthful experiences in Louvain and Bruges, and the pleasure he had derived from those early travels.

Vole was a hospitable man, who would often buy drinks for friends and acquaintances during his lunchtime "sessions" at the Fitzroy Tavern. His conversation often centred around items which had caught his eye in the morning's paper or, in later years, what he had seen on television the night before.

Vole was a keen collector of books, and his small but select library contained many volumes of fiction, history and travel, by such authors as Evelyn Waugh, Daphne du Maurier and D.J. Enright (*shurely shome mishtake? A. W-S*).

During the war Vole retired to Hertfordshire, and his years in Rickmansworth were, again, to provide him with a fund of reminiscence during later periods of his life.

In 1963 Vole moved to a small flat near the Goodge Street tube station, which became his home until his death. In other circumstances, one can easily imagine how Vole's flat could have become a Mecca for the many writers, painters and other luminaries of Bohemia who thronged the Charlotte Street area during those decades immediately after the war. One thinks inevitably of such great names as Keith McBride, Horace Collis and Barbara Fink.

Alas, Vole's genius was not

"I'm afraid we're going to have to let you go, Perkins"

such as to include conviviality among his various gifts, and in later years he rarely saw anyone at all.

Vole was unmarried.

P.F. Vole

Horace Laurence Cartwright Vole, Fitzrovia character. Born Croydon 1923, died Kensal Green, March 1990.

That Heath 40-year lunch menu in full

THE SAVOY HOTEL

Sour Grapefruit Segments

✿

Cold Tongue Pie

✿

Selection of Chips on Shoulder

✿

Bitter Lemon Sorbet

✿

Hard Cheese

✿

Bottle of Vintage 1979 Vinegar

✿

Toast: That Bloody Woman
Proposed by Guest of Honour Rt. Hon. E. Heath

Sheldon Roughtrade

THE DEATH of Sheldon Roughtrade, at the early age of 23, has robbed the world of leather underwear photography of one of its most exciting and outrageous talents.

"Shel" first took New York by storm in 1987, when he rented the foyer of the First Minnesota and Eastern Banking Corporation, to show his daringly voyeuristic polaroids of young men in provocative poses. As Art Ludmilk enthused in his influential column in *Gays and Gaymen*, "these smudgy, unfocussed black-and-white images convey a starkly disturbing, yet deeply arousing synthesis recalling the nightmarish vision of such masters of the homoerotic macabre as Gosch and Boya". Following the success of this exhibition, Roughtrade's work began to appear in many leading fashion magazines, including *Vanity Fair*, *Hullo Sailor* and the Italian quarterly *Uomi*. Some of Roughtrade's friends felt that he had "sold out to commercial values", but it was widely accepted that even in his conventional fashion photography, such as his widely acclaimed series of studies for Damart Thermal Socks, Roughtrade managed to inject a unique note of almost Pinteresque menace.

George Melly

Sheldon Roughtrade was born Melvin Cohen in Hackensack, New Jersey, in 1967. He died in Paris, 6 March 1990.

Lord Rees-Mogg writes: Your obituary of the late Bill Widderspoon, formerly assistant obituary editor of the *Independent*, prompts me to add my own memories of an outstanding member of the *Independent's* editorial team. I shall never forget the day he rang me up in 1988 to ask if I would add a note to the obituary of Sir Halcrow Wainwright, the former Permanent Under Secretary at the Ministry of Agriculture, which he felt had not done justice to an outstanding public servant. I was happy to oblige.

LE EUROPEAN

No.1 WEEKEND MAY 11–13, 1990   EUROPE'S FIRST NATIONAL NEWSPAPER

Voila! Achtung! Good Evening!

'Ici nous sommes enfin,' dit proprietor Robert Maxwell

·

Greatest journal in monde launched

·

'Superbo!' sprach Kohl und Mitterrand

·

Von Nostra Uomo in Brussels ROBERTO DI MAXWELLESCU.

"L'European — c'est moi!"
Señor R. Maxwell hails lui-même et son tremendously exciting neue ventura.

FAITES nein mistake. Dis ist di most fantastico journalistico trionfo in historia di mondi. So dit Herr Robert Maxwellsky, el gran fat idiot Britanique, qui a aujourd'hui launché in London le plus exciting weekly giornale ever seen.

"Le nouveau seminale blat ist printed in 74 colore, avec vorsprung durch technik mit state of the art presses fabriqués en Taiwan," sagt rédacteur-en-chef Roberti Möxwell (keine relation).

Why oh why are we getting so worked up about this greenhouse nonsense?

asks <u>PAUL JOHNSON</u>
WORLD-FAMOUS ENVIRONMENTALIST

SUNFLOWERS blooming on the top of Snowdon. Vineyards in Inverness. Camels roaming the lush savannah of Somerset.

This, we are told, is the nightmare future for Britain if this so-called global warming is allowed to continue.

Keep going

I say, what could be more agreeable? Let us make the most of this new challenge to our ingenuity.

Personally, I can think of no happier picture of the future than being able to sunbathe in a hammock outside my Exmoor cottage, with a large Planter's Punch in my hand, watching the herds of hippopotami gambolling in the limpid waters that lap around the Quantocks.

I see a new vision to inspire Mrs Thatcher as she leads us into the new tropical twenty-first century.

Let Britain's rainforests re-invigorate the ozone layer. Let millions of tourists flock to see orang-utangs swinging from tree to tree through the jungles of Sussex and Hampshire.

More please

They will bring much-needed foreign currency to our shores at just the time North Sea oil revenues begin to dry up.

After all, it has all happened before, as any historian such as myself can tell you. These climatic changes are nothing new.

In Roman times, our ancestors thought nothing of picking wild grapes in December.

In the Middle Ages parrots were a traditional delicacy served at royal banquets.

And in the 18th century, giant turtles sported in the Thames at Hampton Court and were noted by that greatest of all English writers Dr Paul Johnson.

Another 200 words please

Anyway, I don't believe all this doomsday talk about global warming for a minute.

I am told by my distinguished Somerset neighbour, Mr Auberon Gusset, that according to a scientist in California the whole of this greenhouse twaddle has been just whipped up by the media and that there is nothing in it at all.

Once again we can be grateful that Mrs Thatcher has resolutely kept her head, in her determination not to listen to this nonsense and to do nothing at all.

For more than 100 years Sir Jonah Junor was Britain's longest-serving editor. Controversial, waspish, outspoken, he was a legendary figure in his own lunchtime (Shurely 'lifetime'? W.D.)

The night Maggie nearly slept with the entire Cabinet

■ JIM PRIOR was a strange bird. We once had lunch at a leading West End restaurant. He told me an extraordinary story of an incident which had taken place a week or two earlier at Chequers.

It was the night of the great hurricane which devastated much of Southern England. Margaret Thatcher, imperturbable as ever, had gone to bed at her usual hour of 3 a.m.

As the wind howled around the ancient half-timbered mansion set in four hundred acres of the rolling Buckinghamshire countryside (*Get on with it — Ed.*), a gust of wind came in through the window of her bedroom.

So violent was the gale that an old oak cabinet in the corner of the room shook visibly and nearly toppled onto the Prime Minister's four-poster bed.

"So you see," the irrepressible Jim Prior joked to me over his creme brulée, "that was the night Margaret nearly found herself sleeping with the cabinet!"

The strange tale of Edward Heath and the choirboys

TED HEATH had a reputation for being a bit of a loner. As all the world knows, he is not married.

Some say he is a bit of a cold fish. But when I once lunched with a very senior Tory cabinet minister, he told me a story which showed that our bachelor prime minister had another side to him.

During the rehearsal for the annual carol service at his home town of Broadstairs, Mr Heath had dropped his baton in front of the waiting singers.

Some of the smaller choirboys couldn't hold back their giggles. "Oh dear," joked Ted. "I'd better not do that again, or I will be given stick."

I think this charming anecdote shows what a delightful and informal person Ted can be when he lets his hair down.

The day Prince Charles told me of his secret fears

■ I SHALL never forget the day I was invited by Prince Charles to lunch with him at Buckingham Palace.

It was a great honour for me, a humble crofter's son from Auchtermuchty, to be asked round for a tete-à-tete with the future King of England.

I have always had the deepest admiration for this doughty young man, who is never afraid to speak his mind.

When I arrived I was greeted by a smiling footman, who said: "This way, Mr Worsthorne, the rest of your party are upstairs."

When I was shown into the Blue Drawing Room, the Prince came forward to meet me.

"I'm afraid I've forgotten who you are," he said, with an engaging smile. "I'm always terrified of forgetting people's names, and here I am doing it."

How many young men in his position would be so candid in admitting their most secret fears in this fashion?

TOMORROW: Sir Jonah continues his astonishing revelations about famous people he has lunched with.

■ Willie Whitelaw and the Exploding Sausage ■ The Night Sir Alec Lost his False Teeth ■ I Reveal to the World the Secret of the Duke of Windsor's Wig.

Printed on recycled paper

The SUNDAY TIMES

IN THE COURTS

The case was resumed today, before Mr Justice Cocklecarrot, of Neill and Times Newspapers Ltd v. Worthless and the Sunday Telegraph.

SIR RAMPTON BATMAN QC *(for Mr Neill):* My lord, my client, the former Managing Director of the Dirty Digger Dish Co, is one of the most distinguished figures in journalism today. It would be hard to imagine a graver libel than to suggest that such a hugely respected person as Sir Andrew Neill should associate in any way, knowingly, with a lady of easy virtue. And yet this is the allegation that was brought against my client by the defendant Sir Perishing Worthless, in his article "These Bonking Editors Should Be Strung Up", published in the *Sunday Telegraph* on 23rd March 1981.

MR JUSTICE COCKLE-CASSOCK *(for it is he):* Perhaps you could help me, Sir Rampton. I cannot seem to find any mention of Cossacks in the bundle!

(Court erupts into sycophantic laughter at the first, but by no means the last, example of Mr Justice Cockledavies's now legendary wit)

SIR RAMPTON: Mr Neill, would you please tell the Court how you first became acquainted with Miss Pamella Bordello?

MR BRILLO: I remember it well. I had spent a hard day at work writing an editorial for the *Sunday Times* on the inestimable benefits that would accrue to the nation from the introduction of satellite television, and in order to relax I went along to Tarts Club in Filth Street, where I have been a member for several years.

JUDGE COCKITUPAGAIN: I am not sure that I am familiar with the particular establishment you mention. Is it like the Garrick?

SIR RAMPTON: My lord, it is not exactly like unto the Garrick, in that none of the waiters wear ties, or indeed clothes. But, I assure you, my lord, that the regular clientele are persons of the utmost distinction and respectability, including as they do Mr Jeffrey Archer, Mr Spigismond Topes, the well-known popular singer, and Mr Abraham Wargs, the editor of the well known literary review, *Bonks and Bonkmen.*

JUSTICE COCKLECASSOCK: Pray permit your witness to tell his own story, Sir Rampton.

SIR RAMPTON: Indeed, my lord. Sir Brillo, please tell the court in your own words the circumstances in which you were introduced to Miss Bordello.

MR DISH: I was sitting enjoying a glass of champagne, when up to my table comes this delightful young lady of Asian origin. She was, my lord, a vision of unspoiled innocence. I could tell at once that she was of impeccable breeding, outstanding intelligence and would mix without embarrassment with my highly-placed friends in government and the media. And she had terrific tits.

SIR RAMPTON: And what did Miss Bordello say to you?

MR DISH: She said: "Fancy an Indian?"

SIR RAMPTON: And what were your feelings at this moment? Can you recall them?

MR PAD: Indeed I can, your worship. I said to myself, Brillo old boy, this is your lucky night. This little bimbo is a right goer, and no mistake.

MR JUSTICE COCKER-KNICKER: Pray tell me, what is a bimbo?

SIR BRILLO: It is a piece of crumpet, my lord.

MR JUSTICE COCKALEEKIE: A kind of muffin, you mean. We often have them at the Garrick. So these toasted comestibles are also obtainable at the Tarts Club?

SIR RAMPTON: Indeed, my lord. Mr Pad, please tell the court whether you did indeed go for an Indian meal with Miss Bordella?

MR PAD: I did not. Like all good journalists, I made my excuses and came.

(Earlier the court had been read extracts from the leading article in the Sunday Telegraph which had given rise to the action, describing Mr Brillo Pad, and his opposite number Mr "Dirty Don" Trelford of the Observer-on-Thursday, as a "couple of licentious boulevardiers who are in danger of bringing the whole profession of journalism into disrepute". "The duty of the editor of a Sunday newspaper," Sir Perishing had written, "is to dine with the Archbishop of Canterbury or have lunch with the heir to the throne, and never ever to betray the confidences vouchsafed to him by the highest and mightiest in the land. This solemn trust has been flagrantly besmirched by these two salacious spivs in their shiny suits and suede shoes, blow-drying their hair in the lavatories of some of the sleaziest clip-joints in the metropolis, before embarking on an orgiastic odyssey of self-gratification and unabashed hedonism." After lunch the court heard how the Editor of the Observer, Mr Don Juan Trelford, had attempted to win the favours of Miss Pornella Bondes in an effort to boost the flagging circulation of his newspaper)

SIR RAMPTON: Mr Pad, could you tell the court how Miss Bondage rebuffed the pathetic advances of your diminutive rival on the night of 12 February 1986?

MR SKY: I remember it only too clearly, your worship. There we were, in the highly respectable Legover Club, engrossed in a discussion about impact of the Community Charge, when up comes this cocky little bloke with platform heels who says: "Watch out, Andy, there's no such thing as a free dish"

MR JUSTICE COCKYTWERP: This was a reference, was it not, to Mr Murdoch's celebrated televisual device?

(Court erupts into paroxysms of toadying merriment not seen since the celebrated case of Tallstory v. Allalongtimeago)

SIR BRILLO PAD: No, your honour, he was trying to pick up my bird.

SIR RAMPTON: And what was her response to Mr Don Giovanni?

SIR BRILLO: She said: "Would you like a nice Times, ducky?"

SIR RAMPTON: Thereby proving herself a respectable reader of your newspaper?

SIR BRILLO: Exactly.

SIR RAMPTON: And would you say it was an unwise relationship for Mr Trelford to pursue because he was married?

MR BACHELOR PAD: Definitely, your honour. I never did anything wrong. It was all above board.

MR JUSTICE COCKLE-CASSOCK: You mean, "above Bordes", surely?

(Gales of laughter from barristers reach 110 mph)

MR PAD: Right on, your squire-ship. But Dirty Don was two-timing his missus, which to my mind is undermining the whole fabric of morality in our society. I mean, this man is the editor of a respectable Sunday newspaper, the sort of public figure who should be setting an example by having lunch with the Archbishop of Canterbury or the heir to the throne. What is he doing, I ask the court, cavorting around with women of easy virtue? Mind you, he never even laid a finger on her until I'd had my two penny-worth.

MR JUSTICE COCKALEEKIE: Two-penny worth, Mr Pad?

SIR RAMPTON: My client was only, of course, speaking metaphorically, my lord.

(The jury was then asked to retire to consider their verdict)

FOREMAN: What is a "verdict"?

The case continues

AGE CONCERN

More and more old people these days are living in fear of A.N. Wilson coming round to interview them for the *Spectator*. They are old and frail. Their minds may be confused. They may think he is a social worker or a gasman. Before they know where they are, they may have invited him in for a cup of tea and a chat — and in a matter of seconds Wilson has ruined them.

Wilson particularly preys on elderly judges and some members of the Royal Family. But no one is safe.

Armed only with a tape recorder, Wilson worms out of his innocent victims their most intimate thoughts, feelings and prejudices — which he then sells on the Conrad Black Market for huge sums.

If you have reason to think that A.N. Wilson is trying to get into *your* house, here are some simple precautions that you can take:

- **Shut and bolt all doors and windows.**
- **Whatever you do, say nothing.**
- **Call the police immediately.**

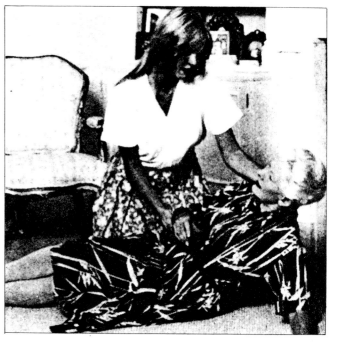

A.N. WILSON IS A SERIOUS MENACE TO BRITAIN'S ELDERLY — BUT TOGETHER WE CAN BEAT HIM

A Taxi Driver writes

A new series in which country cab-drivers are invited to give their views on issues of topical interest.

This week: **Tom Denning**, of Denning's Whitchurch Taxi Service (airports and weddings by arrangement). Cab No. 7.

You see they've let another lot of they IRA bastards out — the Birmingham Six, or the Guilty Four, or whatsoever they may be called? I reckon they was guilty as sin, you know that just by looking at them. No matter whomsoever they are, say I, they must be guilty. I mean, there's no smoke without fire. The only way to deal with people like that is to string 'em up, and then there would be no fretting and fussing about whether they were innocent or no, which they may well have been. Indeed, they presumably were, but that is no reason not to hang them. It's ours not to reason why, that's what I say.

I had that A.N. Wilson in the back of the cab once. He had his tape recorder running, the slimy little German Jew. You know what I'd do with him? I'd string him up.

Here's Micheldever Station now, Sir, and if I'm not mistaken there's your train to London pulling away. Oh dearie me, if I hadn't been going on about this and that we would have caught it comfortably...

NEXT WEEK: Tom Denning takes it all back.

"You'll be hearing from my lawyer"

A Cabby-net Minister writes

Every week a well-known cabinet minister airs his views on an issue of topical importance.

This week: **Nick Ridley** (Cab No. 1939-1945) on Germany and the Common Market.

Take my word for it, guv, you can't trust those Germans. They tried it twice and now they're trying it again with this Common Market. I mean, they're taking it over, aren't they? That bloke, wotsisname, Kohl, just as bad as Adolf, that's what I say. Give it two years and there'll be storm-troopers goose-stepping up Whitehall. I mean, I've got nothing against the Common Market, but when you see that lot in Brussels singing *Deutschland Uber Alles* and telling us what we can and can't do, it fair gives me the hump, I don't mind telling you. Cor, that Leon Brittan. No one voted him in, did they? But there he is, a four-by-two, givin' us our marching orders. If you ask me, that Hitler had the right idea with that lot. I 'ad that Lord Cockfield in the back of the cab once.

***Next week:* Nick Ridley takes it all back.**

By kind permission of Dominic Lawson, Editor of CABS & CABMEN.

How they are related

A.N. Wilson and H.M. The Queen Mother

EGBERT THE FOGEY	LADY MACBETH
ETHELREAD THE SPECTATOR	SHARON OF GLAMIS
CHARLES THE MOOR	THE THANE OF MASSINGBERD
LADY ANGUS WILSON	SIR GORDON OF THAT TONIC
HAROLD WILSON	SIR LYONS CORNER HOUSE
WOODROW WILSON	BEAU DIDDLEY
WOODROW WHYOHWYATT	
A.N. WHYOHWILSON	ADMIRAL SIR MACINTOSH MACINTOSH BOWES-LYON
ANNE WILSON ══	QUEEN ELIZABTEH, THE QUEEN MUM *(Don'tcha love her?)*

Those Ridley-Thatcher letters

Dear Nicholas,

I was deeply saddened when I heard the news that I had sacked you. I shall always be grateful for your huge contribution to the success of this government over the years. I know of no other minister with your integrity, intellect and grasp of foreign affairs. That is because I have sacked them all.

I have decided to fill the huge gap that your untimely dismissal has left with another yes-man whose name escapes me.

Please give my regards to Julie *(Judy? Check name of wife please, Bernard)* and accept my sincere condolences at the unhappy loss of your job.

Auf Wiedersehen,
Margaret Thatcher.

PS: The whole thing was the fault of Hurd and Major. I was all for keeping you until they pointed out it might make me unpopular.

Dear Margaret,

I am surprised after our phone conversation in which you said I could stay on if I apologised, to discover that I have resigned.

I thought I had made it clear that when I gave the interview I was under the impression that I was drunk and that the tape-recorder had been turned off by Nigel's boy while I nipped out to buy a packet of fags.

I now discover that I was sober and giving an on-the-record interview as a Cabinet Minister.

Frankly, I cannot see what the fuss is about. You and I have always seen eye-to-eye on the German question and I was simply spelling it out on the clear understanding that no-one reads the *Spectator*.

However, I do realise that I have no choice but to accept my resignation.

I shall now be able to spend more time with my fags.

Yours ever,
Nicholas.

"Viewers are warned that the next programme has the word 'fuck' in it"

The Alternative Rocky Horror Service Book

No. 94. A Service For Use In Prisons and Other Places Of Confinement.

The Prison Chaplain: Quiet please. We are gathered here this morning according to prison regulations... quiet please...

Chief Warder: Shut your mouth, N or M. [Here he may name any congregant who is talking out of turn, or negotiating the sale of tobacco or it may be some other substance.]

Chaplain: ...As I was trying to say, wherever two or three are gathered together in a cell [or it may be, these days, be seven or eight]...

Chief Warder: ...I've warned you, N or M, you're staring at ten days solitary...

Chaplain: ...Our Lord himself knew what it was to endure God's precious gift of loneliness, which is why, in a very real sense...

All: Kill the screws.

There shall then be some suitable anthem, sung by the congregation, such as "Ere we go, ere we go, ere we go."

Chaplain: Help. This is getting serious.

All: String up the vicar. He looks like a right poof.

First Warder: Jesus Christ, this looks like trouble.

Second Warder: Oh my God, this is it.

All Warders (in unison): Let's push off and watch it on TV later.

THE BREAKING OF THE FURNITURE

Here the congregants shall proceed to the altar and distribute the wine amongst themselves, and shall then break the altar in pieces. The celebrant meanwhile shall then retire to a suitable place of safety.

THE READING

The Ringleader: Right, lads. Basically our demands are as follows. One, we should be released. Two, er...Three. That's it.

The congregants shall then process to the roof where they shall remain for forty days and forty nights.

The Viewers: Send in the SAS.

The Home Office: They shall not be sent.

The Prison Governor: It is all the work of the devil.

The Chaplain: No, well, I think that's being rather literal. I think you'll find the real causes of this unfortunate accident lie in the social conditions prevailing...

He may continue in this vein for some hours.

"She likes people to think she's a drug dealer"

That John Smith City luncheon menu in full

Watered Down Soup

— ❈ —

Scotch Egg Head with Green Salad

— ❈ —

Lobster Claws Four (off)
or
Not Very Red Mullet

— ❈ —

Anti-Thatcher Beef and Gordon Brown Gravy with Half-baked Potatoes
or
Neil Escalope with Treasury Leeks and Hattersley Mange-Tout

— ❈ —

Welsh Rabbits

— ❈ —

Shadow Cabinet Pudding

— ❈ —

A Woman's Right to Cheese

WINES
Red Rosé

— ❈ —

De-Kauffmanated Coffee (Camp)

— ❈ —

*Cigars: Gran Capitalistico Superbo
("just like the Tories smoke")*

KINNOCK LASHES 'MENACE TO BRITAIN'

by Our Industrial Staff
Conrad Blackleg

Labour leader Neil Kinnock yesterday launched what delegates took to be an astonishing attack on NUM President Arthur Scargill.

Without actually naming the miners' leader, Mr Kinnock blamed all the opposition's troubles on "this balding, blustering, empty windbag with his clapped out ideas and his rhetorical diarrhoea".

Delegates gasped as Mr Kinnock warned that Labour would lose the next election "unless this posturing ninny is removed from office very soon".

"We are all sick and tired of seeing on television night after night this pitiful so-called leader, with his bombast, his evasions and his complete lack of any grasp of the complexities of the modern industrial world," Mr Kinnock said.

To a standing ovation, he concluded: "We will only have a real hope of electoral victory when this tired old loser, who is Mrs Thatcher's secret weapon, is chucked onto the scrapheap and replaced by Mr John Smith."

Arthur Scargill is 63.

EXCLUSIVE TO PRIVATE EYE

Mystery of circles solved

by **Nicholas Riddle**
and **Bernie Cornfield**

The enigma of the mysterious circles which have been appearing in cornfields throughout Britain has finally been solved by scientists keeping a 24-hour vigil at the sites.

Explanations of the "paranormal manifestations" have ranged from giant fungi to vortex ionisation caused by abnormal dry wind formations. Other less scientific solutions to the riddle have included visitors from another planet or simply hoaxers.

The Fat Man of Wessex

However, teams of observers working with the very latest infrared cameras last night claimed to have finally cracked Britain's most puzzling mystery.

"It was amazing. It was about three o'clock in the morning," said Professor Heinrich von Hovis from the Zurich Institute of Advanced Wheat Studies. "There were these flashing lights and a noise like a helicopter. Then the craft landed and out stepped this huge larger-than-life alien.

"This figure then walked round in circles, stamping down the corn as he went so that it was completely flat."

Professor Hiram B. Sunblest from the New Dworkin College of Paranormal Bread-Related Phenomena took up the story:

"The Fat Man, as we have called him, spoke in a loud arrogant voice. He was giving orders to his aides, and I recorded a few distinct phrases."

The professor then played his tape-recorder, and the following could be clearly heard:

"This is the ideal site. No one will find it in the middle of the field. We can hide millions of unsold copies of *The European* here. Bring them in the night and dump them."

Robert Maxwell is 103.

REPRINTED FROM THE OBSERVER, 15th July 1990

THAT TRELFORD CITATION IN FULL

SALUTAMUS DONALDIO TRELFORDIO QUONDAM PIXI APPELATUS, EDITORIUS *OBSERVIO* CELEBRATO MULTIS ANNIS CIRCULATIO NOSEDIVUM NOTABILE ET TINI ROWLANDUS ARSLICANDI MAXIMUM ET IN SNOOKORIUM EXPERTUS ET VINO BIBENDUM MAGNUM ET POSTPRANDIUM SOMNOLENS FREQUENTATUS IN GARRICKA CON MULTI VECCIO BORENS ET RELATIONES TANGENTIALES CUM PAMELLA PULCHERRIMA LEGOVERA BORDES. MAXIME HONORI LAUDAMUS DOCTORUS LITTERATUS DISTINCTIS STUPIDUS PARVUS JERKUS PISSPOORUS SACKUM NUNC (*Hoc est satis Trelfordi. Ed.*)

PLANNING

MIKE TURNER.

A Matter Of No Honour

Jeffrey, the tanned, suave and brilliant 50-year-old million-selling novelist, looked across the table at his beautiful, academically brilliant wife, Mary. How stunning she looked as her fragrant blue eyes focused on that morning's *Daily Gazette Herald*. Lady Archer! Yes, that really suited her. And Lord Archer. Perfect, he thought, for a man who had played cricket for England and been in the cabinet at the age of 19.

He thought back to last night when the red phone by his bed had purred like it does in proper novels.

"Hello," he had said…

"Hello." He recognised the voice at once. It was Mrs Thatcher, Prime Minister of England.

"Jeffrey Archer?" she said. "I have good news for you. I am putting your name forward for a life peerage. It is the least you deserve for your years of loyalty and brilliance…"

And now was the time to tell his wife, Mary Archer, the good news about the impending honour.

"Darling," he murmured, "I have some good news."

"What is your good news?" his wife enquired. She looked more beautiful than ever. And he more handsome when he came to think of it.

"The good news," he said, "is that Margaret has given me a peerage. We are going to be Lord and Lady Archer."

"No we're not," she said, "I've just read it in the *Morning Globe*. You've been turned down, along with Rupert Murdoch."

"Damn."

© Somerset Maugham, a woman in Cambridge, a black man in Nigeria and many others too numerous to mention.

■ It is not often that this comic feels obliged to comment on the behaviour of the Royal Family, but it has become apparent from recent nursery rhymes that the monarchy is no longer living up to the high moral standards that we, the nation's children, expect.

Firstly there has been the much-publicised involvement of Royal figures with tarts. The fact that the Queen of Hearts has been frivolously baking tarts at a time of national crisis is bad enough. For the knave to then steal these tarts is even worse. For the King of Hearts to attempt to keep the tart scandal out of the public eye can only be described as disgraceful.

But that is not all. Recent

The Decadent Monarchy

accounts of Old King Cole merry-making in the early hours of the morning while smoking noxious substances in a pipe and being entertained by three fiddling "companions" have again lowered the reputation of the House of Cole in the public's estimation.

The King, in another incident recorded in our sister paper *Mother Goose*, was seen eating a hugely expensive wild-fowl pie containing, according to one witness, a staggering four and twenty live blackbirds. In the midst of a recession such outrageous and insensitive profligacy deserves severe censure.

As does — dare one say it? — Her Majesty the Queen, sitting idly in her parlour regularly scoffing bread and honey. A spokesman for the Palace confirmed the story, but said that the King could not comment, as he was in his counting house, counting out his money.

Surely the time has come for such money to be taxed. Indeed we must go further and insist that the monarchy should in all respects be accountable to its bedtime-story-reading public. And anyone who suggests that these stories are merely fairy tales should try reading the rest of the paper.

© Andy Pandy

Those Howe-Thatcher letters in full

Dear Margaret,

It is with deep regret that I must inform you of my resignation. This unexpected news will no doubt prompt you to ask who I am. I am the one with glasses who sits next to you in the Cabinet — or used to.

I have always been a great admirer of your strong leadership, philosophical vision and ability to sack people who disagree with you.

Your failure to do so in my case has caused me considerable concern, indicating as it does that you have finally lost your grip.

It is for this reason that after sixteen years of careful consideration I have decided to walk out in a bate.

The central issue as I see it is that of Britain's role in Europe or to put it another way my role in the Cabinet. I am in no sense a Euro-Federalist or a Brussels Idealist but I am getting on a bit and I do want to be Prime Minister.

With the political situation so delicate at the moment I am therefore left with no honourable alternative but to stab you in the back and throw the party into chaos.

Elspeth wishes you all the best in your retirement.

Yours,
GEOFFREY
(The one with the glasses)

Bitter, dear?

No, it was a matter of principle

Dear Man with glasses,

It was with great sadness that I learnt from your letter who you were. After 16 years you accuse me of "losing my grip" and I have to concede that you are absolutely right. I should have sacked you in 1979. However, I must at this point pay tribute to your vital role in agreeing with everything I said for 16 years and thus helping me, albeit in a minor way, with my historic triumphs over the evil forces that threatened Britain — Inflation, High Interest Rates, Unemployment and, of course, the EEC.

We shall all miss you, particularly in your role as Deputy Prime Minister which was so vital a post that I have decided to abolish it.

Goodbye and, of course, Good Riddance.

Yours ever
THATCH
(The Supreme Ruler of the Universe)

Dear Fans,

It is with grave delight that I have witnessed the terrible events in the party that I love.

The Prime Minister has proved that, wonderful as she is in so many ways, she is no longer listening to the voice of the party I love.

That voice is saying only one thing and saying it in a calm, sensible tone with a slight speech defect.

We need a man with a vision. A man with a striped shirt and long flowing hair. A man with a vision of himself inside Number Ten with his feet on the desk.

I am naming no names as that would be disloyal at this difficult time and I have no desire to make matters worse.

That is why I am writing this letter in confidence to my constituency (copies to BBC, ITN, *Times*, *Telegraph*, etc).

I would like to make it clear for the 100th time that I do not want to be leader of the Tory Party. I want to be Prime Minister.

Yours unfaithfully,
MICHAEL HESELTINE.

Dear Judas Heseltine,
You're dead, mate.
NORMO TEBBS

(That's enough letters — Ed.)

LETTERS TO THE EDITOR

From Mr Peter Carter-Fuck and Partners, Libel Lawyers to the Rich and Famous

Dear Sir,

We represent our client, the late Mr Sheep, who has become increasingly distressed by the repeated libellous comparison of himself to a Sir Geoffrey Howe.

This has caused my client great embarrassment and has, beyond doubt, brought the reputation of the late Mr Sheep as a leading ex-member of the Grazing Community into grave disrepute.

Mr Sheep resents the gross calumny that he in any way resembles Sir Geoffrey Howe, nor, he points out, would he put up with the humiliating and degrading treatment that the aforementioned Sir Geoffrey has endured at the hands of the Prime Minister for so long.

We thereby give notice that we intend to serve you with a writ for libel within the next seven days unless you agree to apologise to Mr Sheep and pay substantial damages to his relatives or buy a copy of my book, whichever is cheaper.

Yours,
PETER FARTER-CUCK

"Oooh, my anti-hero!"

Code of Practice

We, the undersigned, do hereby solemnly agree to abide by the following self-regulatory code of conduct for now and for ever so long as we shall remain highly important editors of very prestigious national newspapers.

● **A RIGHT OF REPLY. Readers will be entitled, should they feel aggrieved by anything in the paper, to write letters to their hearts' content. These letters shall be given due prominence in the Editor's wastepaper basket.**

● **AN OMBUDSMAN. A senior executive of the newspaper shall be appointed to come in one afternoon a month and empty the wastepaper basket.**

● **PRIVACY. Intrusion into private lives will not be tolerated unless the so doing can be justified as "a cracking good story"** (shurely "in the national interest"? Andreas W-S).

● **MISTAKES. Any errors such as occur from time to time shall be promptly and responsibly repeated in future editions** (shurely "corrected"? A.W-S) **and put in the cuttings library for TV researchers to get wrong.**

● **CRIMINALS. Criminals and relatives thereof will be asked in future to donate their stories for free. However, should they nominate a suitable nominee (i.e. boyfriend of reporter, Fleet Street agency, or man in pub) they may be given huge sums to spill the beans.**

● **RACE. Sorry, no coloureds to be employed on national papers** (shurely "no gratuitous reference to race"? A.W-S).

● **Er...**

● **That's it.**

Kevin Filth, Editor of the *Sun*
Brian Hitchupyourskirtdear, Editor of the *Star*
Wendy Badger (deceased), Editor of the *Sunday Pee*
Sir David Fester, Editor, *The Chequesinthemail*
Charles Gorbals, Editor, *The Wapper*
A Grey Man, Editor of the *Guardian* or possibly the *Sunday Correspondent*
Donald Pixie, Editor, *The Lonrho on Sunday*
Abraham Wargs, Editor of *The Literary Review* (shurely shome mishtake? A.W-S)
Andrew Brillo-Pad, Editor, *Sky News*
Sir Maxwell Hitler, Commander-in-Chief, Allied Forces Dockland
His Divine Holiness The Very Reverend Sri Bhagwash Andreas Whittam-Strobes, Editor, *The Independent* and Convenor of the Grand Board of Born-Again Editors
(That's enough editors. Ed)

New charity craze sweeps Britain!

by Our Comedy Staff
Lord Loon

YES! It's Red Face Day! The day when all over the country senior members of the legal profession put on red faces!

It's all part of the great British tradition known as COMIC RELEASE, an event which is fast becoming a national institution.

What happens is that innocent prisoners are let out of jail, causing huge embarrassment all round.

Last year COMIC RELEASE centred around Guildford, and an amazing four people were freed.

This year Birmingham has done even better and raised the number of innocent men to six!

Said a spokesman for COMIC RELEASE: "Next year it could be hundreds. Who can tell. At this

stonking rate Britain's jails can be empty by the year 2000."

Red Face Day is the brainchild of Lord Lane, who appeared this year with a specially red face to mark his contribution to the success that has been COMIC RELEASE 1991.

Guinness One released

by Our Crime Staff
Anna Ford-Open-Prison

THE controversial "Guinness One" was released from prison today, following an admission in the High Court that he was "definitely guilty".

Mr Gerald Ronson, 53, had been jailed for "making a bomb" in the City, after forensic tests had shown that he had been handling huge numbers of £20 notes.

However, subsequent enquiries have discredited the "£20 note" theory and shown that exactly the same effect could have been produced by handling some totally different substance, such as £50 notes.

Said Inspector Knacker from his Sydney, Australia, hideaway: "This man is definately guilty, which is why he was let out after five minutes. If he had been innocent we would have kept him in for another fifteen years."

UPFRONTERS

☞ Here's a pair of Star Gazzers! Don't cry, Paul, Anne's a real Diamond and she's not going to send you off! Go on, you Brut, and show her your Spurs!

☞ Sue's found a new Desert Island Dish! And Miss Lawley won't Chuck Heston in a hurry! No time for a favourite book, though, with Charlton Athletic! His place or Ben Her's?

☞ Who's Diana Rigged up for this evening? She's remembered to order her Pinter, even if it's only Harold! But which one's the Caretaker?

☞ It's the Hall of Fame! Champagne for Sir Peter, but Sting gets stung for the bill! Everything's going Pop!

☞ Who's driving Nigel Mansell crazy? It's Felicity Kendall, of course, and he's lapping it up! Talk about the Good Life! Keep your eyes on the road, Nige!

Madonna's mad on a new man! It's none other than TV's Charles Moore, deputy editor of the *Daily Telegraph*! Looks like you're a big hit, Charlie, and the Moore the merrier! ☞

☞ Sarah Brightman is feeling a little *horse*! No wonder her singing's suffering! At least she's not saddled with Andrew Lloyd Webber nowadays! That's the Hot Gossip, anyway!

(That's enough piss-poor captions to dreary PR photos by clapped-out hacks — Ed.)

Another case for Perry Worsthorne

The case of the missing readers

ITV 7.45pm.

IN tonight's episode a famous Sunday newspaper loses all its readers overnight. The sinister Canadian-born proprietor calls in Perry Worsthorne and asks him where they've gone. As usual, Perry hasn't a clue.

CAST IN FULL

Perry Worsthorne
. . . . Raymond Burr
Conrad Blackadder
. . . . Rowan Atkinson
Frank Johnson . . . Paul Drake
Moira Fraser Della Street-Porter
Lord Hartwell . . .Alistair Sim
Max Hastings . Richard Wattis
Judge Leroy Davies
. . . . Frank Bruno

10 TELLTALE SIGNS THAT IT'S HOT!

1. Blazing sun.

2. Temperatures soar.

3. No snowdrifts on the M25.

4. Headlines in your favourite Sun newspaper including such giveaway words as PHEW, WOTTA and SCORCHER.

5. Gorgeous dolly-birds tear off all their clothes in a frenzy of heat lust in the street.

6. Shrimps found in lager.

7. Maggie runs amok in reshuffle sizzler.

8. Brains melt.

9. More people than ever buy the scorching, soaraway Sun.

10. Sky-TV wins millions of new viewers as people stay indoors to avoid skin cancer.

 # Apology

In recent weeks, we, like all other sports commentators, editors, and writers, may have given the impression that we thought Cameroon were in some sense unworthy to participate in the World Cup. We may further have appeared to be saying that their presence in Italy was a fluke of the system whereby token Third World clubs were included as a sop to international opinion.

Headlines such as THESE CAMACOONIES ARE LOONIES and WE'LL STUFF 'EM FIFTY-NIL may have mistakenly led readers to believe that the independent nation of Cameroon were, in some way, unskilled in the art of football, becoming excitable in defence and naive in front of the goal, due to their only recent descent from the giant rainforest trees of their delightful country.

We now accept that there was not a scintilla of truth in any of the above and we are happy to make clear that the Cameroons are without doubt one of the most exciting footballing nations to have emerged from this current tournament.

We apologise unreservedly to these Lions of Africa who have shown heart, courage, determination and an ability to lose to England for which we are profoundly grateful.

"Hi, honey — I'm home"

GNOMEBY'S

A Sale Of Very Important Cartoons By Various Hands
Introduction by Prof. Azza Briggs

Few events in the last decade of the 20th century inspired more cartoons than the dramatic decision by Sir Nicholas Garland to leave the *Independent*, the newspaper he had founded and designed, to return to his former position as the World's Most Highly Paid Cartoonist on the *Daily Telegraph*.

Perhaps no cartoonist since Gillray (contd p. 94)

"HOW PLEASANT IT IS TO HAVE MONEY, HEIGH-HO! HOW PLEASANT IT IS TO HAVE MONEY"
(WITH APOLOGIES TO ARTHUR HUGH CLOUGH, BUT NOT TO ANDREAS WHITTAM SMITH)

LOT ONE
(shown above)

—LOT TWO—
"Dropping the Pilot" by Jok. The drawing shows a disconsolate "Kaiser Bill" Whittam-Smith leaning on handrail of the SS Independent while the overjoyed Garland is seen walking down the ladder towards the waiting Telegraph launch.

——LOT THREE——
"If you knows of a better 'ole, go to it" by Gad. The cartoon shows two old soldiers, Cpl "Andy" Whittam-Strobes and Pte Nick "Ideas" Garland, huddled in foxholes in crater-filled landscape while shells full of money explode in background. It is clear from Garland's gleeful expression that he does know of a "better 'ole"!

——LOT FOUR——
"I am going out and I may be some time" by Grud. A small group of dejected-looking and obviously doomed members of the Independent Polar Expedition huddle in a tent. Leaving through the tentflap is a man with a broad smile, Capt Garland, heading for a large limousine with the numberplate MAX 1 standing in the snow outside.

——LOT FIVE——
"Pooh, what a scorcher!" by Scrogg. Pastiche of E.H. Shephard, showing "Pooh" Garland with his paw stuck in a large money jar. Caption: "Isn't it funny how Garland likes money?"

GNOMEBY'S

Author 'profoundly shocked' by own book

by Our Media Staff
Jane Thynne-Stuff

Best-selling author Mr Nigel Nicolson yesterday launched a strong attack on himself for revealing intimate secrets of his parents' love-life in a forthcoming BBC docu-drama *Carry On Sissinghurst.*

"I was shocked," the 73-year-old retired former war criminal said from his Kent home yesterday, "when I discovered that the book contained explicit scenes of steamy lesbian love-bonks involving my parents.

"How on earth could I have written this stuff?" Mr Nicolson spluttered. "It is disgraceful what people will do for money these days. When I published my book *Portrait of a Legover*, it was widely acclaimed as a sensitive and tasteful account of how both my parents were gay.

"But now I find I have sold the rights to the BBC, who are planning to show my father and mother as nothing less than raging homosexuals."

Meanwhile there are also plans to turn Mr Nicolson's book into a musical. Andrew Lloyd-Webber said last night: "We have already come up with the title, *Vita!*, and the rest should be no problem."

Carry On Sissinghurst

Vita Sackville-West	HATTIE JACQUES
Violet Trefusis	BARBARA WINDSOR
Harold Nicolson	KENNETH WILLIAMS
Nigel Nicolson	CHARLES HAWTREE
Head gardener	SID JAMES

Lines On The Passing Of The Right Honourable Margaret Hilda Thatcher, PM

by Sir William Rees-McGonagall

'Twas in the year 1990, on the 22nd of November
That will be a date for everyone to remember.
For it was on that day Mrs Thatcher was forced to resign
After a surprisingly good showing in the first ballot by
                                        Mr Heseltine.

It all began in the House of Commons a few days earlier
When Sir Geoffrey Howe spoke, he had never looked
                                        surlier.

MPs crowded in to hear his historic oration
Which could also, thanks to Mr Baird's televisual
            device, be witnessed by the entire nation.

At his words the Tories were utterly aghast
For they knew now that Mrs Thatcher might soon be
                                        breathing her last.
The Labour Party the Red Flag began to sing.
And Mr Heseltine threw his hat into the ring.

At once the nation was on the edge of its seat
As they watched the inimitable (shurely
            incomprehensible?) John Cole talking in the street.
"Hondootedly Mossis Thotcher," that was his familiar
                                        catch-phrase
Which he was to go on repeating for many days.

At the stroke of 6, the result came through:
Mrs Thatcher 204, Mr Heseltine one, five, two.
Although it seemed that Mrs Thatcher had won
According to the rules, the contest had scarcely begun.

As Mr Heseltine's supporters broke into a dance
The news was relayed to Mrs Thatcher in Paris, France.
She rushed down the steps, after a quick glass of gin
And shouted to Mr John Sergeant: "I fight on, I fight to
                                        win."

Her pledge that she would battle on for another day
Was greeted by senior Tories with dismay.

The members of her Cabinet were soon in cahoots
And Mrs Thatcher had a visit from the men in grey suits.

The message they gave her was loud and clear:
"We appreciate what you've done, but you are no longer
                                        welcome here."
And so it was on the day of November 22nd
Something happened which nobody had ever reckoned.

Mrs Thatcher announced that she would have to go
Which came as a great shock to both friend and foe.
Mr Cole was still talking in the street outside
Explaining that the contest was now open wide.

"Hondootedly," he said, the front-runners would be
                                        Major and Hurd.
The former being someone of whom few had ever heard.
Now the race was on to see who could replace Mrs
                                        Thatcher
While TV's Charles Moore said there was no one to
                                        match her.

For three days there was nothing to be viewed on the
                                        screen
Except the three candidates saying how against the poll
                                        tax they had always been.
The betting shops were meanwhile taking many a wager
As the odds continued to shorten on Mr John Major.

Finally at 6.00 Big Ben began to sound
And Mr Cranley Onslow read out the result of the
                                        second round.
To the astonishment of all the chattering classes
They'd elected some chap in a suit and glasses.

Thus ended an historical chapter in the nation's story,
Bringing a tear to the eye of many a Tory.
Particularly to readers of the Daily Telegraph
While everyone else enjoyed a jolly good laugh.

BRING - BRING

BRING - BRING

OHHH, BRING BACK MY BONNY TO MEEEEE...

◆ THE THATCHER CENTURY ◆

100 GLORIOUS YEARS

SHE was the greatest woman who has ever lived. Of that there can be no doubt (writes TV's Charles Moore, Deputy Editor of the *Daily Telegraph*).

She has been on the throne for so long that no one under 50 can remember a time when she was not Prime Minister.

And in that time she has transformed the world out of all recognition. Just think of her achievements.

Singlehandedly she has wiped out unemployment, inflation and the trade unions.

On the world stage, she has destroyed Communism and brought democracy to countries all the way from Albania to China.

As a working scientist, she has saved the planet from destruction by global warming.

She has singlehandedly united Europe against her.

Her firm stand on the Gulf has forced Saddam Hussein to call her "a demented old cow".

Her firm stand on Northern Ireland has forced Richard Needham to say the same.

At home she is universally loved and respected, as no woman prime minister has ever been before.

It is hard to imagine a world in which Margaret Hilda Thatcher no longer holds sway over the destinies of mankind.

No sooner has she gone than the City is thrown into turmoil, unemployment soars, war seems inevitable in the Middle East and the Four Horsemen of the Apocalypse ride untrammelled across the bleak wilderness which was once, in the Golden Age of Thatcher, a green and pleasant land overflowing with milk and money.

Now there is only one thing left for any loyal Englishman to do. To go into his gunroom, pull down a trusty twelve-bore and shoot himself in the foot.

ON OTHER PAGES

The first solo flight across the Atlantic

The Coronation is seen by billions

Everest is conquered

The four-minute mile is broken

World War II ends with the German surrender

How the image-makers changed John Major

TODAY, more than ever, the world's leading politicians rely on the image-makers to present them in what they call in the trade "the most marketable possible persona".

Just as Mrs Thatcher sought the advice of the Saatchis and Tim Bell to reshape her whole personality, so John Major has followed her example to reshape his.

Mrs Thatcher changed her hair, her teeth, her voice, her clothes — in fact, the 'seventies model bore no resemblance at all to the Thatcher of the 'eighties.

The *Eye* can exclusively reveal that John Major too has quietly been entirely refashioned in preparation for his Prime Ministership in the '90s.

Under the expert guidance of top PR and image consultants Looksgood plc of Richmond High Street, John Major has undergone a dramatic transformation, as our pictures reveal.

We spoke to Mr Gavin at Looksgood, who told us:

"We have worked very hard to produce the John Major you see today.

"Before we got to him he was a walking disaster. Politically, he was a no-hoper. Sandra, my assistant, put her finger on it when she said that in the bad old days he was far too interesting.

"It's been hell, but I think we're now all very pleased with what we have achieved with John in such a short time."

John Major is 47.

June 1985

- Out goes the *Miami Vice* look.
- Out go the Armani suits, the Rayban sunglasses, the designer stubble and the immaculately gelled hair.
- Out go the silk shirts with no tie, the Italian moccasins and the Rolex Oyster.

Jan 1991

- In come glasses from Boots optical counter, suits from Marks & Spencer, shirts from Hornes, shoes from Millets and tie from his mother last Christmas.
- In comes grey-tinged hair, grey socks from his aunt the Christmas before, and Swatch from the London City Airport Duty-Free Shop.

QUEEN'S CHRISTMAS BROADCAST IN FULL

She's gone! Ha! Ha! Ha!

McLACHLAN

Great Moments in Poetry

Ozythatchias
by Percy Bysshe Spartey

I met a traveller on an anti-nuclear demo,
Who told me about those two amazing piles of
concrete,
That apparently exist in the desert that is
Britain today.
The one is a half-finished power station,
Sizewell-B by name.
The other a half-finished tunnel under the sea
near Folkstone.
They both proclaim the legend loud and clear:
"My name is Ozythatchias,
Look upon my works, ye mighty,
And vote Labour."

TEN WAYS TO SPOT THE NEW COCKNEY ARCHBISHOP OF CANTERBURY

1 Talks like Derek Jameson.
2 Wears a cloth cap under his mitre.
3 Supports the Gunners.
4 Will crack down on Pulpit Pooftahs.
5 In favour of ordaining Page 3 lovelies.
6 Likes Dire Straits and Chas 'n' Dave.
7 Has Bible printed on recycled paper.
8 Owns rottweiler called Satan.
9 Eats whelks.
10 Widely respected scholar and theologian (*shurely shome mishtake? Ed.*)

THAT BR SNOW IN FULL
— telltale pictures released

by Our Rail Staff **Liverpool Street-Porter**

BRITISH RAIL today released pictures showing the two types of British snow, one of which resulted in wide-scale disruption during the recent "Siberian snap".

A BR spokesman said that research would be carried out at the BR Institute of Snowology to try and find a way to convert the dangerous new killer snow into the old-fashioned commuter-friendly nonexistent snow.

Thomas The Tank Engine has been cancelled due to adverse weather conditions.

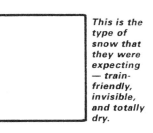

This is the type of snow that they were expecting — train-friendly, invisible, and totally dry.

This is Killer Snow — white, damp and fallen from the sky.

10 THINGS YOU NEVER KNEW ABOUT A.S. BYATT

1. Her real name is A.S. Byatt.
2. She was once married to the famous Water Board official Horace Byatt.
3. She has written 5,412 novels, many under pseudonyms such as A.S. Byatt and Anton Bruckner *(Surely 'Anita Brookner'? Ed)*.
4. Her father was the well-known judge Mr Justice Drabblecarrot, who once asked: "Who is A.S. Byatt?"
5. Her nickname in literary circles is Bazza.
6. She has a pet mutant terrapin called Fra Angelico.
7. She has a morbid fear of appearing on *The Clive Anderson Show*.
8. When she was a little girl she once went to the seaside.
9. Er...
10. That's it.

SHREE ANDREAS WHITTAM-BHAGWASH

This saintly figure first rose to prominence in the late 1980s when he set up his famous "school of boredom" in the City Road. Attracted by his other-worldly aura and his doctrine of supreme dullness, thousands of followers flocked to join his movement. His mystic utterance "It is. Are you?" seemed to sum up a wholly spiritual approach to life that made an especial appeal to young, affluent, middle-class whites looking for a meaning to their existence. His disciples, known as "The Grey People", were distinguished by their colourless suits and short hair. They included many famous journalists, amongst them Adam Mars Jones, Stephen Glover, Peter Jenkins and Miles Kington.

"To see Shree Andreas seated at his daily 'editorial conference' discoursing on a topic such as 'The Money Supply', 'The European Regulatory Mechanism' or 'Lawson's Economic Miracle' was to feel oneself in the presence of a charismatic, almost divine figure," wrote worshipper Alexander Chancellor.

Yet in the early 90s the dream began to go wrong for the "San Andreassyn", as the devotees were known. Shree Andreas himself grew richer and more remote. He took to making frequent foreign trips leaving the running of the ashram to his less capable subordinates who began increasingly to quarrel amongst themselves.

He began new ventures, including a newspaper for children to indoctrinate them early into his philosophy. And then finally he overreached himself, spending millions of pounds on a gigantic monument to his movement — the *Independent on Sunday*.

It was a sad end to one of the greatest religious figures of the late twentieth century.

by Stephen Glover (formerly an aide and bodyguard to the Bhagwash)

Shree Andreas Fotherington Whittam Strobismus, 1987-1990

'Everything appalling' — Prince's shock claim

by Our Royal Staff
Antonia Holden-Guest

In a shock series of speeches yesterday morning, Prince Charles lashed out at a number of things that he described as "really appalling".

Among the Prince's latest targets were:

● **Those Wimbledon strawberries** — *"Bloody expensive — something should be done."*

● **Train strikes** — *"Every bloody week... something should be done."*

● **Hay fever** — *"Bloody pollen everywhere... someone should act."*

● **Sir Michael Tippett** — *"Why can't anyone compose bloody decent tunes anymore?"*

● **England's cricket team** — *"A bloody disgrace... heads should roll."*

● **Paul Johnson's why-oh-why articles** — *"Wonderful how he manages to find 12 new things to attack every day."*

THE KINGSLEY AMISH MEMOIRS

Sir Kingsley Amis, novelist, critic, wit, philosopher and drunk, has bestridden literary life for seventy years. Now for the first time Sir Kingsley looks back over the crowded decades and can't remember anything of interest because he was drunk all the time. Read these amazing extracts from The Book of the Year

The day Roald Dahl was rude to me

I SHALL never forget the day I met Roald Dahl, or was it Enid Blyton? Anyway, one of these absurd children's writers who make a lot of money. "Hullo, Kingsley," he said, "you're looking well." There was no mistaking the malice behind his fatuous pleasantries. What the fellow was trying to tell me was that I was overweight and that my last novel was a lot of tosh. "Well," I replied, quick as a flash, in the lavatory twenty minutes later, "that Postman Pat is full of shit." That put him in his place.

The night I met T.S. Eliot

I SHALL never forget the night I went on the piss with T.S. Eliot. First of all we got legless on brown ale in that pub in Soho which I can't remember the name of. Then Eliot said he knew of this place in Hampstead where there was plenty of birds and booze, so we got in a cab, which of course I had to pay for, despite the fact that he was rolling in money because of his piss-awful poems, which didn't even rhyme. He said he'd come out without his wallet. Ha, ha, ha, they all say that. So when we got there it was yours truly, as per usual, who had to shell out the 7/6. No, I tell a lie, there was also the tip, another 2d. Mean bastard. I can't say I remember much about the rest of the evening except that poor old Tom got brewers' droop when confronted by Tom Driberg in a tutu. Or was it Desmond Tutu in a driberg? Never mind, Tom may have been a bloody useless writer, but he was a good bloke to have the odd jar with.

Why I hated Dylan Thomas

I SHALL never remember the day I met this disgusting old drunk in a pub in Swansea. He was loud, bad-tempered, self-pitying, lecherous. He spent the whole evening telling everyone what a great writer he was, and how useless everyone else was. Somebody said: "Do you know who that is? It's Kingsley bloody Amis." "Don't be a fool," I said. "It's Philip Larkin, or is it Enoch Powell, or Anthony Powell, or Malcolm Muggeridge, or Charles Dickens?" What a shit *he* was, by the way, filthy rich and never paid for a round in his life. I never thought his poems were any good. Anyway, it doesn't matter. The important thing to remember is, er... mine's a Teacher's, old boy, make it a treble. I'm afraid I've forgotten my wallet...

NEXT WEEK: My night of passion with Mrs Thatcher, the world's sexiest woman.

"You've swallowed a fly, perhaps you'll die"

Rushdie — renewed calls for fatwah

by Our Islamic Staff
Alan Koran, Minaret Marin and Allah Watneys

THE long-running saga of controversial novelist Salman Rushdie, author of *The Satanic Verses*, **took another dramatic twist yesterday when there were renewed calls for the fatwah declared against him by the late Ayatollah Khomeini "to be implemented immediately".**

The calls came from Dr Youssef Mohammed Ali Akhbar Islam ben Muslimwallah (formerly the novelist Mr Salman Rushdie), speaking from a secret television studio in London.

The recently converted Dr Muslimwallah explained that, as a devout Muslim, he was deeply offended by certain chapters in his own book, which he described as "a blasphemy against all that is sacred in Islam and a crime against Allah".

He called the author "lower than the dogs" and declared that it was his solemn duty to kill himself at once.

"There is no possible forgiveness," he said, "and there is no point in Mr Rushdie trying to hide."

"I will catch you in the end," he told himself. "The game is up."

Cat Stevens is 45.

Who's Who in the New Yugoslavia

As Yugoslavia slides towards civil war, *Private Eye* prints a handy cut-out-and-keep guide to the personalities who are shaping the destiny of tomorrow's Balkans.

SLOBODAN DANISLOB, 47, charismatic leader of the Serb New Democrat Party (formerly the Communists), whose calls for the extermination of all Croats in Kosovo has recently provoked mass demonstrations in the autonomous region of Prin by irredentist Bosnians who are demanding the massacre of the Hercegovinian minority in Slovenia led by Montenegrin-born Mihail Kuthisballsov, 41, whose Croat-led anti-Communist militia is accused of plotting a bloodbath against Albanians living in the largely Orthodox, Muslim-speaking Pristina stronghold of the *(continued p. 94)*

NODDY'S NEW LOOK

BY Enid Ryton

It was a lovely sunny day and Noddy climbed into his car. "Hello," he said. "This NUCLEAR POWER NEIN DANKE sticker wasn't here yesterday. How strange! I don't remember it being a Citroen Deux Chevaux either", he thought as he drove along the Old Bruce Kent Road into Toytown.

The first person he met was Mr Tubby Bear.

"Hello Mr Tubby Bear, you fascist bastard," he found himself saying. "How dare you wear fur? Take that!"

And little Noddy poured red paint all over Mr Tubby Bear.

"Gosh. I feel a bit different today," he thought as he turned the corner and was waved down by WPC Plod.

"Where's Policeman Plod?" he asked.

"He was sent down for racially harassing Golliwog," the woman policeperson told him.

"Golly!" Noddy exclaimed.

"Right. You're nicked as well."

Oh no! Everything seemed to have changed to poor Noddy.

"You have the right to one phone call," said WPC Plod.

"Alright," he said, unable to stop himself picking up the toy phone. "I'll phone Esther. Hello Esther? It's about Big Ears. He's a perv."

"Good little Noddy," said WPC Plod. "I'm letting you off with a caution."

So Noddy went on his way and who should he see next but Sailor Doll?

"Hello, Sailor," he said.

"That's it Noddy!" interrupted Sally Social Worker (née Skittle). "That's the last time *you* introduce gay stereotypes into this story."

"Oh dear, Noddy," said Mr Macpathetic, the Publisher. "I'm afraid you haven't been revised enough. We're going to have to replace you with someone more socially acceptable who reflects the country's changing cultural fabric in a multi-plural society."

Chapter Two

Mohammed Al-Akbar Noddwallah left the mosque and cycled home for tea and hot toasted copies of *The Satanic* (Continued Page 94)

Puffins seized in dawn swoop

**by Our Men in the Hebrides
S. Johnson and J. Boswell**

HUNDREDS of social workers were yesterday parachuted onto the unin-habited Scottish island of Mugg, where they took "into care" three guillemots, four **puffins and seven sheep.**

Said Roz McWimmin, 42, Co-ordinator for the Strathclyde Social Services Child Abuse Outreach Unit: "We have very good reason to believe that these animals have been subjected to Satanic rites and ritual abuse."

"I cannot understand this at all," said the island's lighthouse keeper, Jimmy McFraggle, 82. "We've never known anything like this on Mugg before. But we've all got to move with the times, and I'm sure these social workers know what they're talking about."

(Pompous music, expensive graphics of storm clouds gathering over world capitals)

JEREMY FAXMAN: On day 94 of the great Gulf Crisis, President Bush stands firm. Jordan's King Hussein looks for a compromise. Saddam moves up his Scud missiles. And Norway sends in her navy.

(Shot of old car ferry sailing down fjord, captioned "Library Footage")

FAXPERSON: Later on I'll be joined by the Iraqi ambassador in Paris, Mr Yesman Deafaid *(picture of man with moustache looking shifty)* and from New York, Walter Dullberg, who under President Ford was Deputy Assistant Adviser to the US National Security Council. Also, we shall have a couple of gratuitous interviews with the relatives of some hostages. But first, the moment you've all been waiting for, Peter Snooze in the sandpit. Peter.

(Cut from man in silly tie to man in ill-fitting suit standing in front of very badly made papier mache model of Lake District with sand sprinkled on top and labels stuck on, reading, "Baghdad", "Amman" and "Mrs Thatcher")

SNOOZE: Just look at the hardware that the Americans are still pouring in to the Gulf area. In the last 24 hours alone they have brought in 73 aircraft carriers, most of them over 100,000 tonnes, 16 World War Two battleships, including the recently refitted USS Watergate, not to mention several thousand cruisers, destroyers and nuclear-armed submarines. *(Empties box of toy battleships all over blue areas)* And then there's the air power — 840 of the latest Stealth bombers, 3,500 F-194's — they're the ones fitted with the deadly accurate Correspondent seek-and-miss air-to-ground missiles that were used to take out Col. Gadaffi's tent. *(Dive bombs Lake Windermere with plastic plane)* And then here along the Saudi border *(climbs onto model)* they've already got the 98th Airborne Tank Marine Corps under the 57-year-old Vietnam veteran Col. Sanders, whose men were feared throughout South-East Asia as "the Finger Lickers", because they couldn't lick anything else. Now, with me, I've got General Sir Anthony Farrer-Gussett *(shot of elderly white-moustached man in crisp blazer standing to attention)*. General, the Americans have now got the biggest build-up of military power the world has ever seen. What are they going to do with it?

GEN. SIR FARRER-HACKETT: It all de-

SNEWS NIGHT

with JEREMY FAXMAN and PETER SNOOZE

pends on Saddam. He's in a corner and he knows it.

SNOOZE: So does that mean he'll use his chemical weapons in a first-strike deployment? *(Sets fire to Scafell Pike with lighter, filling studio with dense smoke)*

GEN. HACKETT *(spluttering)*: Saddam is no fool. But nor are we. And if Saddam wants to play the germ card, then I can tell him here and now — and I know he's a keen watcher of your programme — we've got all it needs to hit him, and hit him pretty damn hard.

SNOOZE *(Now peering through smoke from inside NBC-CBS protection suit)*: So are you saying that we would respond by using our nuclear capability?

(Model disintegrates, Faxperson's tie catches fire.)

HACKET *(still standing at attention amid rubble)*: We've got a full range of options, but I'd be a damn fool to tell you what they are.

SNOOZE: Thank you, General, and now back to Jeremy.

(Faxperson sitting at desk amid large pile of chemical foam from fire-extinguisher)

FAXPERSON: As the international chess-game escalates, I am joined on the satellite-link by the Iraqi ambassador to Paris, Dr Hussein Aziz Cakeandeatit.

FAXMAN: Dr Aziz, you've been telling us a lot of lies in the past few weeks. What have you got for us tonight?

AZIZ: Sorry, I cannot hear very well. We Iraqis have an age-old tradition of hospitality. Our Western guests will be shown every consideration during their long stay in our lovely country.

FAXPERSON: Now listen here, towel-head, when you say guests, don't you mean hostages?

AZIZ: I can't hear you. Our guests will be picked up at their homes by specially trained armed couriers, and taken to specially selected 5-star chemical hotels.

FAXPERSON: Where they will be used as human sandbags and given nothing to eat... Isn't that the scenario, you horrible little Arab creep?

AZIZ: I'm sorry I didn't hear that question. Our guests will enjoy food every bit as good as that eaten by our beloved leader President Hussein. *(Takes out menu card and reads)*

The Saddam Sizzler

Grapeshot Segments or Fruit Jews

———

Filet of Beef-Iftytwo

or

Steak Tornados with Mustard Gas Sauce

or

Cockpit Au Vin

———

*Followed by Arabian Dessert
Bomber Surprise
Tea or Coffin*

FAXPERSON: That's in very poor taste, Ambassador.

AZIZ: No, it's delicious.

FAXPERSON: Now, Ambassador, if you could just stay with us, we're going to have the American view from Walter Dullberg, who was once on President Carter's staff as Chief Director of Desert Hostage Rescue Operations. Dr Dullberg, how do you read President Bush's statement today that "in no eventuality should anyone imagine that we shall not respond with a proper reciprocal strategy to any situation which may develop, and that is fully covered by Article 94 and Resolution 726 of the United Nations"?

DULLBERG: Good evening.

PACKMAN: Sorry Professor, that's all we've got time for. And now, a quick look at tomorrow's headlines. The *Sun* front page leads with GAZZA SIZZLES IN 90° SCORCHER. *The Times* goes with PAUL GASCOIGNE ADMITS IT IS VERY HOT and the *Financial Times* has BRITISH GAZZA TO BE PRIVATISED. Oops, I've forgotten all about the hostages. Never mind, we'll have a double helping of them tomorrow and we'll hear their views on why President Bush should sue for peace. From me and Peter Snooze, it's goodnight.

(Camera tracks away to reveal Snooze buried up to his neck in sandpit, still gibbering about battleships)

Your Cut Out and Keep Guide to Who's Who in the Middle East

SADDAM HUSSEIN, President of Iraq, Kuwait (possibly more).
Ambitious, intensely able, charismatic mass-murderer. Even his opponents would admire him if they were still alive. Voted Moustache-Man-Of-The-Year 1987-8-9-90 by Baghdad's leading facial hair magazine *Moustaches and Moustachemen*. Clubs: huge ones with nails in them.

SHEIKH HUSSEIN AL JOLSON, present Prime Minister of Kuwait Province, Greater Iraq.
Small, ambitious, intensely related to his brother-in-law Saddam Hussein, who gave him Kuwait as a surprise 21st birthday present. When in Kuwait City he would not like to meet the members of the 82nd US Airborne Division.

SHEIKH RATTLE-AN-ROLL-OVER, little known Emir of the Trucial Arab Protectorates (TAP).
Sheikh Rattle has made his position towards Iraqi dominance of the Middle East unequivocally clear. It's fine by him, so long as they let him keep his 79 Rolls-Royces and his 16 houses in Berkshire and allow his wives a Gold Card Shoplifting Facility in Harrods.

SALMAN-AL-RUSHDIE, exiled novelist, whereabouts unknown.
Ambitious, hugely rich author of *Salman the Helicopter and Other Tales*. When in London he would like to be able to walk down the street.

SYRIA
Baghdad
IRAN
JORDAN
KUWAIT
SAUDI ARABIA
EGYPT

KING HUSSEIN, King of Jordan (at present).
Small, intensely frightened Old Harrovian. Keen admirer of Neville Chamberlain. When in Baghdad would like to lick boots of above. Hobbies: legover.

SHEIKH HUSSEIN-AL-OVER-FOR-ME, deposed ruler of Kuwait.
Small, depressed, intensely broke former strong man of oil-rich Kuwait. Has personal assets estimated at 0.38p. Now loitering within-tent somewhere in Saudi desert. When in Kuwait would like to be back in power.

HUSSEIN-AL-MUBARAK, President of Egypt.
Large, intensely shifty Arab statesman who has made his position unequivocally clear by expressing strong condemnation of the US 6th Fleet by allowing it to sail through the Suez Canal.

SIR MARM-AL-ADE HUSSEIN, Ruler of the BBC.
Large, moorhen-loving, affable autocrat who has ruled BBC with a rod of iron since the dramatic coup of 1987 in which his predecessor, Al Asdair Milne, was forced to abdicate. When in London would like to be in Somerset, particularly in this hot weather.
(That's enough Arabs, Ed.)

THE Sun

WE FLY OUT THE PAGE THREE GIRLS!

KILL A TOWELHEAD AND WIN A TRIP TO DISNEYWORLD

THE SUN SAYS

BASTARD!

Bastard, bastard, bastard. Bastard!

Bastard, bastard, bastard. Bastard, bastard, bastard. Bastard! Bastard, bastard, bastard.

Bastard! Bastard! Bastard.

Bastard, bastard! Bastard, bastard, bastard. Bastard! Bastard, bastard, bastard. Bastard, bastard, bastard. Bastard! Bastard, bastard, bastard. Bastard!

Bastard! Bastard. Bastard, bastard! Bastard, bastard, bastard! Bastard! Bastard!

Bastard! Bastard, bastard, bastard. Bastard! Bastard, bastard, bastard. Bastard, bastard,

ON OTHER PAGES: Bastard!

The Foreign Office guide to spotting a World War about to break out

1. One million men in uniform with guns are sighted massing along the border of someone else's country.

2. The leader of that country has a moustache.

3. The man with the moustache makes speeches saying that the smaller country next door has rightfully belonged to his country for hundreds of years.

4. Gooch scores triple-century at Lord's.

5. Temperature soars into 90s.

6. Mysterious corn-circles appear in Wiltshire.

7. Queen Mother celebrates 90th birthday.

8. Angela Rippon's marriage hits rocks.

9. You decide to go on holiday.

10. World War breaks out.

THE ALTERNATIVE ROCKY HORROR SERVICE BOOK

No. 94: Christmas Day Worship for Troops Stationed in a Muslim Principality

Recreation Officer *(for it is the padre):* Peace be with you.

All: Until Jan 15th anyway. *(Or they may name some other date in accordance with UN Resolutions.)*

Recreation Officer: Allah be praised.

All: Death to Rushdie.

Recreation Officer: We are all gathered together at this time of celebration to give thanks to the Father Christmas for sending so many presents into the world.

All: And to the *Sun*, for sending us so many individual Ramadan puddings.

READING

(From the Koran or from the Harrods gift catalogue, whichever may be deemed more appropriate. For example the following may be read):

"Let not your women be seen topless for it is an abomination in the sight of Allah. Let no alcoholic beverages pass your lips because that too is an abomination. He who drinketh and driveth his camel shall be stoned to death. Happy Allahmas!"

THE CAROL

There shall then be sung a suitable carol from the Cat Stevens Hymnbook, e.g.

"While shepherds watched their flocks by night,
All seated on the ground
Dee dum dee dum dee dum dee dum
This chap Mohammed is jolly sound."

Recreation Officer: Morning has broken.

All: As indeed has war.

Man in the News

Our Man at the UN — Sir Potato Crispin

Potato Orlando Cervantes de Crispin Crispian seems at first sight to be an unlikely man to be co-ordinating the efforts of the 167 nations of the free world to bring down the mad dictator of Iraq. But in the last ten days Sir Potato has emerged as the most

accomplished diplomat on the world stage this century.

At the UN headquarters in New York, diplomats from all over the world speak of him with barely concealed admiration. "He is an English gentleman of the old fool," said one Peruvian official.

Until his present post as Britain's number-one UN troubleshooter, Sir Potato was best known for the immensely able way in which he conducted the tricky negotiations over the 1984 Costa Rican red bean dispute.

He first came to the notice of Mrs Thatcher with his seminal memo in 1989 arguing that something ought to be done about these hot summers we've been having.

Since he was posted to New York, Sir Potato has perhaps become best known for his habit of presenting his guests at diplomatic dinners with salads made from dinosaur eggs and poisonous fungi collected from Central Park.

Today, make no mistake, Sir Potato is the most powerful man in the world, which is why in three days' time he is due to retire.

"... and in the studio with me tonight to discuss the military strategy is Johnny Thompson, who once owned an Action Man!"

GAZZA — aren'tcha sickofhim?!?! Wherever you look there he is with his gappy teeth and his dopey grin!?!?? OK, so he cries??!! Who doesn't?! I tell you, Mister, I cry out loud every time I hear his stoopid name?!?

Take a tip from Auntie Glenda, Cry-Baby Bunting — get yourself a seat on the subs' bench and stay there for the rest of the season?!? Gazzzzza (Geddit?!)

LEAVE HIM alone!?!! Gazza, I'm talkin' about, stoopid!?! He's only a kid, for gawd's sake!!? So give him a break, and stop hypin' this handsome hero before it's too late!?! What he needs is time to grow up without the newspaper know-alls tellin' him how to live his life!?!

Belt up, everyone, we've all heard enough about Gazza!!!?!

GAZZA?!?! About time he got himself a new dolly-bird!?! What's the matter. dearie?! Don't you like girls?? We'll be calling you Gayzza next!!? Geddit?! (Obviously not!?! Geddit?!?!!)

GAZZA?!?!! *(We've had him — Ed.)*

GLENDA SLAG

She's hotter than the Gulf!

JAZZA?!?! Jilly Cooper to you?!? She's the upper-class madam who writes raunchy books about toffs bonking!?! Wanna laugh?! Now Jazza's hubby Leo has been havin' it away behind her back?!? Just like in her books?!! Except now you can save yourself a fiver and read it all in the papers for 22p!!?

LAZZA?!?! Leo Cooper, I'm talkin', about, dumbo! What a swine?!? How could he two-time one of the kindest, sweetest, most generous, loving,

warm, affectionate, compassionate, attractive, intelligent, charming friends of mine in the world?!?

Do us a favour, Lazza!?! Buy Jilly a bunch of flowers and tell 'er that you've been a bad boy!! Oh, I nearly forgot! Tell Scarlet Sarah, your bit on the side, to throw herself off a bridge!!?!

COME OFF it Mrs Parnes, Mrs Ronson and all those leggy blonde daughters!!?

So you knew you'd be on the front pages with your thighs a-showin' and a-glowin'??!? Next time your old man's being banged up, why don't you come along in your birthday suits?!??!

HERE THEY ARE, Glenda's Kuwait Kuties!?!?
● **KING FAHD.** You may have 350 wives already, Big Boy, but there must be room for one more?!?
● **GERALD RONSON.** So they've put you in an open prison?!? Makes it easier for this little gal to get in at nights!!? Mmmm…
● **WILLIAM WALDEGRAVE.** Crazy name, crazy guy!?!

Ciao!!!

APOLOGY

To His Holiness the late Ayatollah Khomeini of Iran
Over the past ten years, in common with all other newspapers, we may inadvertently have given the impression that the late Ayatollah Khomeini was the most evil man in the world, a vile tyrant and the gravest threat to world peace since Adolf Hitler.

We may also have given the impression that President Saddam Hussein of Iraq had in some way been worthy of our wholehearted admiration and support in his gallant 10-year struggle to rid the world of the menace of the Ayatollah. We further may from time to time have indicated that we might in some way have approved of the sale of western arms and technology to President Hussein, on the grounds that these were being used to further the entirely laudable purpose of eradicating the wicked old lunatic with the beard and thus making the world a safer place.

We now realise that the late Ayatollah was in fact a saintly and scholarly cleric whose only concern was to save the world from the evil clutches of the Hitler of Baghdad, the wickedest man in the history of the world, Mr Saddam Hussein.

We would therefore like to apologise to the late Ayatollah and family for any distress that these articles may have caused.

Heath's mercy dash 'Why I did it'

by Our Sour Grapes Staff
Sid Bitter and Russell Twisted

An angry Grocer Heath today rejected suggestions by Mr Douglas Hurd that he was only flying to Iraq as a publicity stunt.

As his one-man mission prepared to leave London, he told reporters: "My sole motivation in this matter is one of humanitarian concern. It is ridiculous to suggest otherwise."

Asked why he had chosen the middle of the Tory conference to announce his bid to bring peace to the Middle East, Mr Heath said: "The timing was purely accidental. I could not sit back and do nothing any longer.

"I am only thinking of a poor old man in the evening of his years, cut off from everyone, with nothing to do all day but sit and count the hours.

"What has he got to look for-

"Bore-Bore is better than War-War"

ward to? It is an affront to civilised values to ignore his desperate plight.

"I say, let me go now — so that I can make life difficult for that awful woman. She is another Hitler. and unless we stand up to people like that we will have failed to learn the lessons of the last war."

GULF WAR — Eye Picture Probe

Where Britain's intelligentsia stands

Lady Magnesia Freelove, historian and hostess

War is always horrible. But there are times when it can be justified. For instance, when the Sandineasdas overthrew the American-backed dictatorship of President Samosa. If you want my full views on this you'd better speak to my husband.

Harold Pinter, the world's greatest living ex-playwright

The Americans are bastards. Just look what they did in Grenada, Panama, Nicaragua and Vietnam. Where was the UN when the Sandinistas got voted out of office? No bloody invasion then. Bastards.

Dr Jonathan Miller, Renaissance man and uomo universale

As Noam Chomsky has rightly said, war is a terrible thing, particularly when the Americans are involved. It was the great 17th-century Belgian anatomist de Krooning who once said "De bello non est disputandum." Kafka, I am sure, would have agreed.

Margaret Dribble, the world's greatest novelist

I blame this war on Mrs Thatcher. It was her bellicose warmongering that got us in this mess in the first place. I believe people will eventually agree with me that this war is a human tragedy almost as bad as the poll tax. The sooner Mrs Thatcher resigns the better.

Mohammed Al-Haroun *(formerly the novelist Salman Rushdie)*

I am right behind Iran on this one, wherever they stand, and support their impressive and statesmanlike leader Rafsanjani. All praise to Allah.

Sir Perishing Worthless, voluptuary and libertine *(shurely 'philosopher and political commentator'? Ed)*

Lying on the pillows at the home of my fiancée Lady Embonpoint, I try to think of un bonne point (!) to make in my column. War can be a beautiful thing. Very like love. You make love, you make war, you make it up as you go along. I say the allies should nuke Baghdad now.

Rabbi Lionel Blue, rabbi and broadcaster

Hullo Brian, hullo Sue. You know, when I woke up this morning I felt ever so gloomy, what with all the news about the war. But then I remembered a little song my granny used to sing to me during the Blitz. How did it go? *"When the clouds are grey, and bombs are in the air, then drink a bowl of chicken soup and say a little prayer."*

Sir Auberon Wargs, autobiographer and oenophiliac

Why should we fight for a bunch of randy towelheads, led by His Excellency Prince Mahmound-al-ben-Mustafa-Fukh, the 73-year-old hereditary ruler of wherever it is? Some ghastly little hole in the desert without a decent bottle of claret to be found anywhere, full of stinking camels covered in weeping sores. To hell with the lot of them, that's what I say.

Continuing our round-the-clock, extended, non-stop, continuous, ball-by-ball coverage of the Gulf War.

DAVID DIMBLEBORE: I'm sorry, I must stop you there, Admiral, because we're just getting in reports of a possible missile alert at Ahzid-Ahrain, which is in... er... eastern... er... General, do you have any comment on that?

GENERAL SIR HORACE GUSSETT: Well, I think we've got to be very cautious about this one. At the moment this report, if there is one, is unconfirmed. You'll remember we had a similar report yesterday that three AF-79s had been sighted further up the coast, and of course later in the day we got further reports which seemed to show that the earlier reports had been...

BRIAN REDHEAD: I'm sorry to interrupt you, General, but we're just going over live to Martin Bell, who is at a forward base somewhere in Saudi Arabia.

(Still picture of man in flak jacket talking on telephone)

KATE ADIE *(for it is she):* Hullo, Brian. We're getting unconfirmed reports here that you've been getting reports of a possible missile attack on an as-yet-unidentified military target somewhere in the Middle East.

BRIAN: What is the mood there, Kate, wherever it is you are?

BRIAN BARRON: Well, you have to remember that it's three o-clock in the morning out here, so the mood is pretty quiet, due to the fact that everyone is asleep. Of course I cannot say too much, and I cannot reveal exactly where I am, but I can tell you that if a missile were to land anywhere near here we'd certainly know about it.

JEREMY PAXMAN *(in studio):* Admiral, I come to you first. You were listening to that. What do you think we can really say about the mood here in the studio?

ADMIRAL SIR RODERICK GUSSETT: Well, of course, the first thing we have to remember is the weather. At this time of the year there's a lot of it about, particularly in that part of the world. This makes forward operations very difficult, which may be why we are getting these reports.

PETER SNOW: I must stop you there, because I just want to show a video of the type of missile we believe may have been responsible for this attack, if one has taken place.

(Cut to out-of-focus film of rocket being fired into the sky. Caption reads "MANUFACTURER'S VIDEO")

SNOW: The great point about the PF-34 Scorcher missile is that it has a range of 2,000 miles, and can only be brought down by the new American Asskicker anti-missile missile, which has not yet been invented.

DIMBLEBORE: Thank you Peter, but I must interrupt you because we're going over live to a replay of the press conference given earlier today by Marlon Rotweiler of the Pentagon.

ROTWEILER: Good day, gentlemen. I have to announce that we have this morning received reports, as yet unconfirmed, of an Iraqi missile attack on military targets in the area of Ahzid-Ahrain. We are unable to give you any further information at this time. Yes, Jim?

REPORTER: Jim Pipesucker, *Idaho Chronicle.* Can you tell us the exact time planned for the launch of the allied attack on Kuwait?

ROTWEILER: I'm sorry, Jim, but at this moment in time that information is classified.

NAUGHTIE *(in studio):* Paddy Ashdown, you've been listening to that briefing in Washington. How do you think it is going to affect the mood in the House of Commons? Can the cross-party consensus be held, do you think? After all, it is four days since the vote when, as you know, there were 23 Labour abstentions.

ASHDOWN: Well, let me say as a former commando...

NAUGHTIE: Sorry, I'm going to have to cut you short there, because we are going over live to Tel Aviv and our reporter Julian O'Halloran. Julian, what are the Israeli papers saying this morning about these latest reports of a possible missile attack on

Ahzid-Ahrain? Is the Israeli policy of restraint still holding?

O'HALLORAN: The mood here is sombre. Of course, if these attacks had taken place on Israel, then I need hardly say that the mood would have been even more sombre. Hold on, I think something is just coming through on the television.

(Crackly pause while O'Halloran asks colleague what is on the television)

O'HALLORAN: Well, it seems that a senior Defence Ministry spokesman here, General Moishe Golan, has just refused to comment on the possibility of any direct Israeli response to the reports of the missile attack on Ahzid-Ahrain.

FRANCINE STOCK: Thank you, Julian. We'll be back to you later, but before we can confirm those reports about the latest possible missile attack let's just have one more look at the film of the laser-bomb attack on the Baghdad defence ministry which we've all enjoyed so much.

(Blurred black and white film, somewhat worn from endless replaying on all channels, showing square building falling apart. American voice-over: "Holy cow, it works!")

PAXMAN: It's time now for my nightly sparring match with the man we all love to hate, Mr Alfalfa Ahmed Fawsis, the Iraqi ambassador in Paris. Mr Towelhead, what lies have you got for us tonight?

SHIFTY-LOOKING MAN WITH MOUSTACHE: We're going to murder your prisoners of war. What do you say to that, English dog?

PAXMAN: You bastard. Thank you, Ambassador. And now we're going over live to the House of Commons to hear the concluding stages of this afternoon's debate on the Gulf.

ELDERLY MAN IN GLASSES *(reading from paper)*: ...and can my Right Honourable Friend now make a full statement on the shocking reports which have been carried on the BBC today, about a possible missile attack on the town of Ahzid-Ahrain, where it may well be that there are a great many defenceless women and children and a large number of British expatriates. Can my Right Honourable Friend assure me that, if these reports are in due course confirmed, the response of the allies will be swift, firm and, above all, swift?

DOUGLAS HOGG: May I say at once that the Government takes these reports very seriously indeed...

HONOURABLE MEMBERS: Hear, hear, z-z-z-z-z...

HOGG: ...and I can give a firm and unequivocal assurance that, if these reports turn out to be confirmed...

NICHOLAS WITCHELL: Well, we have to leave the debate there, because it's time for un update on those unconfirmed reports about a major missile attack on

Ahzid-Ahrain. But first, what kind of impact is this war having on the taxi-drivers of London as they ferry a mighty army of retired admirals, generals and air marshals round the various radio and television studios?

POLLY TOYNBEE *(standing in street with rain falling)*: Every day, literally hundreds of retired senior officers are being summoned to London from all over the West Country to appear on Gulf Special radio and television programmes. Naturally this is putting an almost intolerable strain on London's already hard-pressed taxi service. With me is Mr Russell Twisk, editor of *Cabs & Cabmen*.

TWISK: On behalf of my members, I would like...

(Cut back to studio)

DIMBLEBORE: I'm sorry to cut you short there, Polly. I'm sure we'll have time to come back to you later, but we're now going over live to the Gulf where there are unconfirmed reports that General Norman Schwarzkopf may be about to give a press conference.

(Cut to still picture of Bob Simpson and John Simpson watching TV screen in hotel in Amman)

JOHN AND BOB: Hullo, David, yes, we can confirm that General Schwarzkopf's press conference is being broadcast by CNN at this moment.

ALASTAIR STEWART *(in front of palm tree in Saudi Arabia)*: Can I just break in there to say that I've just had a call from ITN's Mike Nicholson with the Royal Navy in the Gulf to say that he's watching CNN as well.

(Cut to CNN)

GEN. SCHWARZKOPF: Gentlemen, the war is going exactly according to plan in every particular. That is all I can report to you at this time.

REPORTER: Don Eagleburger, *New Dworkin Bee*. General, can you confirm reports of a rocket attack on the location of Ahzid-Ahrain?

SCHWARZKOPF: All I can say is that there has been no attack, and there is no such town.

DIMBLEBORE *(back in studio)*: Well, Air Vice-Marshal, we've heard that absolutely categorical denial from the Supreme Allied Commander of the reports we were picking up earlier about the missile attack. Where does that leave us?

AIR VICE-MARSHALL SIR HUMBERT GUSSETT: Well, we've filled up twelve hours...

DIMBLEBORE: I'm sorry, Air Vice-Marshal, I'll have to cut you off there, because we've got unconfirmed reports that we may be able to go back live to a taxi-driver for his assessment of the Gulf War so far.

SID GUZZA *(cab no. 8842)*: ...that Saddam Hussein — know what I'd do with 'im? String 'im up. That's the only language people like 'im understand.

DIMBLEBORE: I've got to stop you there, because we're now going to show you all of this Gulf Special again...

(Continued all day and every day on all TV and radio channels)

"Is there honey still for tea? And are there tits still on Page Three?"

THE BOOK OF SHAMIR

Chapter 194

1. And it came to pass that when Sad-dam had been reigning in Babylon for eleven years, he rose up and marched with all his host against the land of Ku-wait.

2. Then did all the nations wax fearful and did gather together to cast out the Saddam-ites from the land of Ku-wait.

3. And Sad-dam pondered in his heart how he might divide all those nations that stood against him, even one from another.

4. And he sayeth unto himself: "Behold, there is one thing which will set my enemies against each other, as surely as the ensnared scorpion of the desert stingeth itself even unto death with its own tail.

5. "If the children of Israel can be goaded into joining in, then verily will the Arab-ites and the Syrian-ites and the Egyptian-ites and all those that weareth the towel upon the head, then shall they unite against the children of Israel, the American-ites, the Briton-ites and all the infidel sons of Un."

6. And he told all these things unto CNN, even unto Peter, son of Arnett, who hangeth upon every word that issueth from the mouth of Sad-dam.

7. And then Sad-dam descendeth into the very bowels of the earth, even 200 cubits deep, to a place which is called Bun-Ker, which is to say made in Brit-ain.

8. And when he was hidden in that place privily, he ordered forth the mighty weapons, which are called Scud, to fall upon the children of Israel like unto the fire and brimstone which descendeth from heaven upon Gomorrah.

9. And it came to pass that the Scuds rose up and fell by night upon the tents of the children of Israel. And there was much wailing and gnashing of teeth.

10. And Shamir waxed wroth and cried aloud, saying "Verily, this requireth a smiting such as the world hath never seen. For is it not written that we should give an eye for an eye and an Scud for an Scud?"

11. But when the American-ites heard these words, they were sore afraid. And they begged Shamir, even upon their bended knee, that he should withhold his arm from the smiting and exercise restraint.

12. And Shamir mocked the American-ites and answered them, saying: "Who are we, the children of Israel, to show restraint? Were we restrained when the Arab-ites fell upon us in 1948 and 1956 and 1967 and 1973 and 1982?

Where would restraint have gotten us then?"

13. And, lo, even as he spoke, there was heard, like unto a mighty rushing wind, another Scud descending upon the city of Tel Aviv.

14. And the children of Israel spake unto one another, saying: "Lo, Sad-dam hath sent unto us another Scud, so low indeed that it hath made an hole 10 cubits wide and 12 cubits deep."

15. And Shamir said unto the American-ites: "Wherefore should we show restraint? For what good hath it done us? Verily, I say unto you that the hour hath come for the smiting to begin. And the cities of Babylon shall be as dust. And the people of Sad-dam will cry out for mercy."

16. And once again the American-ites waxed sore afraid. And they took counsel amongst themselves and cometh up with an bright idea, namely to send to Shamir a mighty engine of war which is called Patriot.

17. And Shamir looked upon the Patriot, and saw that it was good.

18. And Shamir cried out to them: "Lo, I am almost restrained, but for just one more thing. The children of Israel are poor, and our children have no bread.

19. Just cast your eyes upon the beaches of Eilat, for they are as empty as the sands of the desert. For the Sons of Thom cometh not to ride upon the boards of surf and to drink the coladas of piña. So what suggesteth thou with regard to this one?"

20. And Shamir holdeth forth his hand, and giveth an wink, saying unto them: "See how restrained I am. For the Scuds raineth down upon us night and day, and yet I hold my peace."

21. And at last the American-ites getteth his drift.

22. And, lo, from that day forth the coffers of Shamir were filled with much gold.

23. And all the nations of the world payeth tribute to Shamir, quite a lot of tribute as it happeneth, for that he was wondrously restrained.

24. And when the American-ites and the Britain-ites and the German-ites and the Nippon-ites had all paid him, even an hundredfold, then Shamir said in his heart "Yippee!", which is to say this one hath been an nice little earner.

25. But he also saith unto himself: "The day hath nearly come when the children of Israel shall sadly be forced to cast off restraint, like an old garment, and get on with the smiting."

Here endeth the Lesson.

ALLIED TROOPS SUCCESSFUL IN SUPRISE ATTACK

by Alfred, Lord Tennyson of the Crimea News Pool

[*This despatch has been compiled under reporting restrictions*]

Units of the British Light Brigade today directed a major assault on Russian artillery positions.

Unconfirmed reports have been received that our troops advanced at least "half a league", despite encountering severe fire from the enemy ordnance on both right and left flanks.

The valley into which a large number of coalition troops charged cannot be named, but it is believed to be somewhere near Sebastapol.

Despite sustaining "minor casualties", the Brigade secured all its objectives, said a spokesman at a press briefing in Constantinople.

Asked whether the British brigade had made "a number of tactical errors", the spokesman said: "It was not theirs to reason why. They were there to do a job. The Crimean War is running exactly according to schedule."

Lord Raglan is 153.

"It's a Mirage . . ."

THE FIERY ORB

THE PAPER THAT SUPPORTS OUR BOYS

Ascensiontide. The Year of Our Lord Eleven Hundred and Ninety Two

The Orb: First with ye illuminated manuscripts

Sod Off Saladin!

From the News Pool in the Holy Land
John, Son of Simp and Kate A.D.

THE coalition forces of Flemish, Frankish and English troops today continued their aerial bombardment of the city of Acre.

With the new hi-tec ground-to-air catapults they are confident that they can remove Saladin from the disputed territory without a prolonged crusade.

"Everything is going to plan," said the head of Allied Christendom Command, "Stormin' " Godfrey de Bouillon, "but it could take longer than expected, possibly up to seven centuries, to recapture the Holy Land."

"Our main worry," continued Godfrey in a lengthy briefing to learned clerkes, "is that Saladin may set fire to the oil and then use it as a chemical weapon to be poured against ground forces."

He ended by imposing restrictions on all chroniclers as he said the speed of media reporting was now such that detailed accounts of battles were reaching home within three years.

THERE'S MORE FUN IN THE FIERY ORB

"Because of events in the Gulf, children's programmes are cancelled again. So, instead of 'Sesame Street', we now go live to the Gulf . . ."

"Here I am in a convoy of tanks — there are 1-2-3-4-5 tanks in front of us and 1-2-3-4-5 —TEN tanks . . . um . . . ELEVEN tanks . . . and oh wow! look at those BIG RED ROCKETS! 1-2-3 rockets! Each of those rockets is bright red, six-feet long, weighs a ton and costs six squillion pounds . . . Listen to the weird noise they make . . . there they go — 1-2-3 rockets! Wheee! Wheeeee! Wheeeee!"

The *Guardian* is proud to reprint the column about the bias of the British press that helped it win the coveted What The Papers Say award for Nwespapre of Teh Yare.

Propaganda in British Newspapers

We have...
The American War Machine

We have...
Pentagon Hawks

Our missiles cause...
Horrific civilian casualties

Our support for Israel is...
Hypocritical

George Bush is...
Warmongering

Macho

Imperialist

We ignore UN resolutions...
Cynically

We have...
Censorship

Disinformation

We at the Guardian are...
Insufferably smug and
self-righteous

They have...
Teenage Conscripts

They have...
Senior Revolutionary
Commanders

Their missiles cause...
Embarrassment to the Coalition

Their attacks on Israel are...
Inevitable

Saddam Hussein is...
Being painted into a corner

Not being allowed to save face

Clearly willing to withdraw

They ignore UN resolutions...
In a spirit of compromise

They have...
Reporting restrictions

Official sources

Everyone else is...
Stupid and evil

(That's enough Grauniad — Ed.)

It's not about oil

That Gulf coverage in full

Day 194

BRIAN REDHEAD: ... and there are unconfirmed reports of a very serious battle indeed raging somewhere that we cannot talk about for security reasons. We'll come back to that as soon as we know even less about it than we do now. General, I wonder if we could pick up on what we were saying four hours ago, about what is going to happen when the war is over.

GENERAL SIR ANTHONY FARRER-GUSSETT: Yes, well, that is the main question now. There's no doubt that we've got a whole new range of problems to cope with here. What I'm thinking of in particular is what is going to happen to all these hundreds of generals; air vice-marshals and other experts who are going to have to pick up the pieces of their lives. I mean, what is perhaps difficult for the non-military mind to grasp is what it is like when, for nearly six weeks, you've been there in the front line in one studio after another, facing a continual round-the-clock barrage of questions about things you know nothing about. You never know when the next topic is going to land on you — and then suddenly, it's all over. A deathly silence. Nothing but the clock ticking in your study as you sit there all alone doing the *Telegraph* crossword and wondering when the lady wife is going to come in to say that lunch is ready. War is a grisly business — but nothing like as gruelling as peace.

REDHEAD: I would like to bring in a leading expert on depression here, Dr Anthony O'Looneigh. Doctor, you've made a special study of what you call the Post-Conflict Withdrawal Trauma Syndrome. Would you say that some of the most serious casualties of a modern war are those experts who find that after a period of intense nervous excitement and being at the centre of world events they cannot readjust to normal post-war life without extensive counselling therapy by highly-trained experts? And would you further say, in the light of your studies, that in extreme cases it may be necessary to administer large amounts of scotch whisky ...

O'LOONEAIGH: Can I come in here?

REDHEAD: No, you may not, I do the talking on this show.

The Lynn Babar Interview

HELLO DALAI!

He looks like a saintly mystic, but is he a raving sex-fiend?

"HOW OFTEN do you get your leg over?" I ask the bespectacled self-possessed spiritual leader of Tibet's seven million Muslims. The Dalai Lama gives an enigmatic smile and smoothes his orange robe with a gesture of sanctity. Or is it shiftiness?

"Come on, Dalai, tell us about the women in your life. It can't all be sitting around in a monastery contemplating your navel."

Once again the so-called Holy Man will only give a wry smile. Friends had told me that he was likely to be reticent, especially on the subject of sex.

"Are you a poof, then?" It is not an unreasonable question. A lot of monks are that way inclined, and there is no reason to believe that the Dalai Lama is not in fact some sort of robe-lifter, as other friends have indicated.

There are few clues to be garnered from the room in which he holds court. Two chairs (one for his boyfriend?) and a photograph of a monastery. The tea he offers is hot and sweet.

"Is that how you like your women, then?" I ask. "Like your tea?"

The dark side of the supposed Living God is immediately in evidence. He offers me more tea and smiles in a sinister fashion. What a creep, I think *(cont. p.94)*

"Damn it, batteries in the wrong way round!"

brian bagnall

"They're sleeping together"

The Kurds
– an apology from The Rt. Dishonourable Douglas Hurd

In common with all other politicians, we the British Government may from time to time in recent months have given the impression that the genocide of the Kurdish people by President Saddam Hussein was a crime of international importance, and a major justification for our going to war with the "Hitler of Baghdad".

Statements such as "Remember Halabje?", "Saddam — The Kurd Killer" and "Why This Proud People Must Not Suffer Any Longer" may have suggested to the Kurdish people that their being gassed by President Hussein was a matter of concern to people in the West.

We now acknowledge that President Hussein is fully entitled to do anything he likes to the Kurds or indeed anyone else within his borders. We further acknowledge that if he wishes to kill hundreds of thousands of Kurdish citizens, this is none of our business, and is a matter for him and him alone, which is all that is likely to be left of Iraq by the time he's finished.

DOUGLAS KURD
Foreign Secretary

Scene: The Drones Club

(There is a sound of low droning from various members of the Cabinet. "Biffy" Patten is throwing bread rolls at "Barmy" Mellor with a lot of giggling. Camera zooms in on "Bertie" Major staring at period copy of Daily Telegraph headed MAJOR COCK-UP OVER KURDS*)*

BERTIE: Oh, I say. I seem to be in a bit of a fix with regard to these Kurd birds.

BARMY: What ho, Bertie! You look a bit glum.

BERTIE: Oh yes. I jolly well am. These dashed Kurds. They get a chap down.

BARMY: Why don't you have a word with your man Hurd. He went to Eton. He'll come up with some wheeze.

(Cut to Hurd brushing down suit with deferential expression)

HURD: Do I take it Sir is concerning himself over the slight matter of the displaced Kurdistanis?

BERTIE: Yes, I jolly well am, Hurd. I mean, dash it, no one at the Drones had even heard of the little blighters until yesterday. Not even "Stiffy" Waldegrave, and you know what a swot he is.

The new Sunday night comedy sensation starring Stephen Fry as **HURD** and Hugh Laurie as **"BERTIE" MAJOR** plus the late Hermione Gingold as **AUNT MAGATHA** in

HURD AND MAJOR
by P. G. Wodehouse

HURD: Yes, sir, you are referring, I take it, to the unfortunate mountain-folk of northern Mesopotamia, who were regrettably not given independent status in the Lausanne Settlement of 1921.

BERTIE: Yes, alright, Hurd. That's enough of your history lessons. But what am I supposed to do now? That's what I want to know.

(Phone rings. Hurd answers it. He listens for some minutes as loud voice of elderly female can be heard squawking down the line)

HURD: Very good, ma'am. I shall convey your instructions to Mr Major at once.

(Replaces receiver delicately)

HURD: That was Lady Thatcher, sir. She wishes you to know that she is much exercised by your apparent failure to come up with a solution to the Kurdish problem.

BERTIE: Dash it all, Hurd! Give a chap a chance. I was about to come up with something, just as soon as you'd told me what it was.

HURD *(polishing silver teapot)*: It did occur to me, sir, that since these unfortunate people had to leave their homes because of our intervention, perhaps we should intervene again to escort them back to their homes.

BERTIE: Brilliant, Hurd! I say, what an absolutely top-hole notion! You wouldn't have a name for this scheme of ours, would you?

HURD: Might I suggest, sir, that since the essence of the plan is to persuade these unhappy Kurds that they will find a safe haven from all their adversities, we should perhaps entitles the project OPERATION SAFE HAVEN?

BERTIE: Good Lord, Hurd, I think you've got it!

(He moves to piano and sings, to his own accompaniment "Haven, I'm in haven..." Hurd grimaces at appalling travesty of old song and resumes polishing silver)

CHRISTMAS FILMS

CHRISTMAS EVE
BBC 2 9.00 a.m.
THEY FLEW TO BRUGES
(1948 black and white)

Hardy wartime perennial in which a group of undercover resistance fighters fly to Bruges. Spirited performances by David Niven as the young Lieutenant and Richard Attenborough as the Chief Steward. Jane Thynne provides the love interest as the army nurse stranded behind enemy lines. Directed by Eric von Hamburger.

BBC 8.30 p.m.
B.T.
(colour, 5 hours)

First ever TV showing of Steven Driberg's classic 1982 sci-fi fantasy. Alien creatures invade the telephone system and create worldwide havoc. People get wrong numbers and huge bills whilst others make a fortune. Maureen Lipman stars as harassed housewife Mrs Yehudi Menuhin, who is trying to phone her son Melvyn and keeps getting the Chinese restaurant. "Arnold Schwarzenegger impresses as the Rabbi," writes Barry Norman.

"You might as well get mother out now as well"

CHRISTMAS DAY
ITV 3.00 p.m. and 7.00 p.m.
WHO KILLED MRS FOTHERGILL?
(made for TV, 1989)

Inspector Pisspoirot (Peter Ustibequitefunny) returns in a two-part special to investigate the mysterious death of elderly heiress Mrs Fothergill in her luxury retirement home on the Caribbean island of St Bruno. All her houseguests come under suspicion as the inspector grills them in the conservatory. Who is the killer? Is it actress Jenny Seagrove (Nicola Pagett) who is married to ageing film producer Michael Winner (Albert Finney)? Or is it her faithful butler Gielgud (Leo McKern)? Or is it... *(That's enough suspects, Ed.)*

BOXING DAY
Channel 4 11.00 a.m.
DUDLEY 7
(1984)

Hugely unsuccessful sequel to *Dudley 6* in which cuddly comedian Dudley Tesco (Arthur Moore) goes to Hollywood and gets married to several actresses in quick succession. Co-starring leggy Californian blonde Bo Peep as the psychiatrist.

BBC1 3.00 p.m.
LAWRENCE OF ZHIVAGO
(1972)

David Lean's classic masterpiece in its original uncut 7-hour version starring Omar Sharif as the Bedouin doctor from Moscow who keeps up the troops' morale as they build a bridge over the river Danube. "Cast reads like a Who's Who of cinema greats," writes TV's Barry Norman. Peter O'Toole as the alcoholic Sheikh Jeff Bin In. Julie Christie as the young Agatha Christie, who finds herself caught up in the maelstrom of the Cossack repatriation. Alec Guinness in his controversial role as Nelson Mandela, a young South African lawyer defending Gandhi (Ben Elton) against the wicked Czarist troops.

BOXING SUNDAY
ITV 9.00
GERBILS
(1987 colour)

Based on Stephen King's horror classic, a small mid-west town, Garrison Keiller, is terrorized by mutant gerbils when a nearby chemical research station mysteriously blows up. Horrific special effects by George Lucasade include a giant gerbil eating its way into the stomach of a pregnant woman and then devouring the foetus. Family fun. Stars Ronnie Elfin and Jamie Lee Rusbridger as the kids who take on the gerbils. Fine cameo by Burt Lancaster as kindly patrolman Kloog.

(That's enough rotten films, Ed.)

PROGRAMME HIGHLIGHTS

CHRISTMAS EVE
BBC1 11.00 p.m.
CLIVE JAMES MEETS SANTA CLAUS

Hard-hitting interview in which the waspish critic and intellectual Clive Jaws probes the secrets of the world's most hated man. What does he have for breakfast? How many reindeer has he got? How does he keep his beard so nice and white?

CHRISTMAS DAY
ITV 11.00 p.m.
NIGEL KENNEDY AT CHRISTMAS

Live from Coventry Cathedral, the world's number one violinist plays *The Four Seasons* and selections from *The Four Seasons*. Plus Autumn, Summer, Winter and Spring by Vivaldi, and a special spot where Nigel introduces his favourite melodies from Vivaldi.

BBC 1 3.00 p.m.
THE QUEEN

Esther Rantzen talks about child abuse with reference to the Christmas story. Should the Messiah have been taken into care?

(That's enough Xmas TV, Ed.)

THE GREATEST NOVELIST WHO EVER LIVED

BY ANTHONY BURGESS

It's the Jaci Stagg column

GRAHAM GREENE first met me in 1957. It was a memorable occasion, especially for him. I had just finished my first brilliant novel and Greene was desperately jealous about the way I had written about Catholicism, which he considered his own territory. This did not make for a good start in our relationship, particularly as my books are so much better than his and sell so many more copies.

Greene was always a prickly man and resented any criticism of his books. I once wrote to him to say that on page 249 of the 2nd edition of *The Power and the Glory* one of the characters had ordered Earl Grey tea from the Lyons Corner House, Fulham Road, in 1936. Anyone with any knowledge of the pre-war Fulham Road would have known that Earl Grey tea was not available at Lyons until three years later.

Greene very rudely acknowledged my letter, thanked me for my observations and promised to correct them in future editions. He added as a PS that he had hugely enjoyed my latest book, *Incident In Penang*.

He did not, needless to say, make any such alteration in subsequent editions, which only goes to show how much his claims to greatness have been exaggerated.

The incident of the Earl Grey tea was to lead to the final estrangement between Greene and myself. This took place in 1963, when I called on him in his house in Antibes to ask him what he thought of my latest best-selling and critically acclaimed masterpiece, *Incident in Kuala Lumpur*. I asked him in addition whether I could quote him on the jacket of the paperback.

With an apologetic smile, Greene confessed that he had not yet had a chance to read my book. He had the effrontery to tell me that he was very busy at that moment finishing a novel and would probably not have time to read my book for several days.

This was blatantly untrue since all the world knew that Greene could only write a paltry 200 words a day, compared to the output of some truly great novelists. I am thinking of one in particular, who knocked off *Incident In Seringapatam* in Serbo-Croat in less than an afternoon (and wrote a symphony while he was doing it).

It was a matter of great sadness to me that I had to tell Greene what a talentless little creep he was.

Now he is dead he must be thinking how fortunate he is that all the newspapers and TV programmes have asked me to pay tribute to the greatest novelist of the twentieth century — myself.

She's new!
She's Welsh!
She's dirty!

MEN'S BUMS? Don't-chaluv'em?! They're big! They're bouncy! They're beautiful!

Cor!! When I see a fella's bum a-wigglin' and a-squigglin' I sure get the hots mister and it kinda drives me wild!!

(You're fired. Ed)

"Watch out — it's slopping out time!"

PILBROW

"I'm afraid I've overspent my drugs budget again, Mrs Jones"

Lines on the 70th Birthday of the Duke of Edinburgh

by Mr Ted Hughes, Poet Laureate

Old Pit Bull
Snarls on leather
Leash. Brass studded
Teeth bared. Jaws slaver.

Old Himmler waits.

Tied to lamppost
On dirty street.
Owner lager-filled in
Sweaty pub.
Sawdust feet, NF tattoo
On flexed muscle.
Torn T-shirt.

Old Himmler broods.

Leash slipped,
Old Himmler away.
Pounding, padding.
Jaws lock,
Biting fury, trousers rent.
Mr Patel taken to Casualty.

Old Himmler does it again.

Happy Birthday,
Your Royal Highness.

T.H.

'THE DAY I REALISED IT WOULD COME OUT'

IN THE comfy chaos of her Gloucestershire home, Jolly Sooper talked frankly to me (and sixty other hacks) about the terrible trauma she has just lived through.

"You never think it's going to be you," she said sadly, patting her favourite Labrador on the head. "And then the terrible phone call comes.

"My stomach churned, the room seemed to spin, and I felt a terrible guilt and rage and depression and shame and anger."

She is quiet for a moment, lost in the bitter memory of how her country idyll was shattered by one brutal phone call.

"It was my publisher. He said: 'It's going to come out tomorrow.'"

"What? The terrible truth?" I asked. Jilly shuddered as she recalled the day of reckoning.

"'No,' he said. 'Your book. *Polo*. It's coming out. We've organised a press conference. So you can do your weepy number about Leo's bit on the side.' I was horrified, and agreed immediately. It's appalling what a woman has to go through in order to make a lot of money. Even discussing her private life just to drum up a few sales at airports. It's humiliating, really."

There was scarcely a dry eye as Jilly posed for photographs in front of her agreeable stone fireplace and handed out a press pack entitled 'JILTED JILLY'S DAY OF ANGUISH'.

Jolly gave us a last wan smile before ushering us to the door.

"Thank you so much," she said. "You've all been terribly sweet and kind, but now I need some time to be alone with the television crew that's coming to interview me."

© JollySooperTrash

TODAY'S TV (all channels)

7.00	Inspector Morse
8.00	Inspector Wexford
9.00	Inspector Van der Valk
10.00	Inspector Poirot
11.00	Inspector Maigret (rpt)
12.00	Inspector Columbo
1.00	Inspector Sherlock Holmes
2.00	Inspector Miss Marples
3.00	Inspector Lovejoy
4.00	Inspector Spender
5.00	Inspector The Sweeney (rpt)
6.00	Inspector Taggart
7.00	Inspector Morse

(That's more than enough detectives. Ed.)

TV Highlights
Thursday, BBC2, All Night

The Marriage of Figaro
The controversial new production from Glyndebourne, set in a police station in Oxford. Inspector Figaro investigates how Mozart has been hijacked by yet another idiot setting it in a ludicrous period.

CAST IN FULL

INSPECTOR FIGARO	Janet Baker
SERGEANT CHERUBINO	Robert Tear
CHERUBINO'S MISSUS	Dame Kiri te Kanawa

Friday, Channel 4, All Night

Il Nazi di Figaro
The controversial new production from Glyndebourne, set in a Harlem occupied by the Nazis, with Obergruppenführer Figaro and MC "Cool" Cherubino, the rapper who *(That's enough terrible opera. Ed.)*

Where Were You When Kennedy Was Assassinated?

EVERYONE can remember exactly where they were when they heard the news that Radio 3 Chief John Drummond had assassinated the character of popular, charismatic violinist Nigel "Nige" Kennedy.

The world was stunned when the loner Drummond struck his fatal blow from the fifth floor of the BBC gramophone record depository at Broadcasting House.

For three years Kennedy had caught the imagination of the younger generation with his good looks, his energy, his unconventional style and his refusal to bow down to the Establishment.

Famous quotes fell from his lips, from "Ask not what I can play in in your country — you're getting the Four Seasons" to the now legendary "Ich bin ein Berlin Philhamoniker."

But then came the terrible day when, for reasons which still remain a mystery, the crazed Radio 3 Chief fired his lethal shot.

"Kennedy is a wonderful violinist and a very good friend of mine. However he should get his hair cut and buy himself a proper suit. Honestly, he looks no better than those people you see in the King's Road on Saturday, when you're shopping for croutons."

Where were you when this historic event took place? Let us know, on a postcard, and win 100 free tickets to Radio 3's Festival of Contemporary Music at St. John's Smith Square, 24 June.

How They Are Related

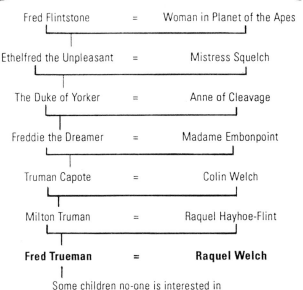

Fred Flintstone	=	Woman in Planet of the Apes
Ethelfred the Unpleasant	=	Mistress Squelch
The Duke of Yorker	=	Anne of Cleavage
Freddie the Dreamer	=	Madame Embonpoint
Truman Capote	=	Colin Welch
Milton Truman	=	Raquel Hayhoe-Flint
Fred Trueman	**=**	**Raquel Welch**

Some children no-one is interested in

The Daily Telegraph

181 MARSH WALL LONDON E14 9SR TEL: 071 538 5000 TELEX: 22874/5
TRAFFORD PARK MANCHESTER M17 1SL TEL: 061 872 5939 TELEX: 66

A Tragedy For Africa

THERE can be no cause for rejoicing in the downfall of Mrs Winnie Mandela. The fact that the wife of the deputy leader of the African National Congress should have been sentenced to six years' imprisonment for kidnapping and assault should give no pleasure to those who have the best interests of all the peoples of South Africa at heart. The spectacle of the "Mother of the Nation" being found guilty of crimes against her own people, including dedicated campaigners against the evil of apartheid, is one from which no one of goodwill can draw any comfort.

Certainly this very unhappy personal tragedy must not be allowed in any way to influence our view of Mr Nelson Mandela, the deputy leader of the African National Congress, who throughout this sad affair has comported himself with the utmost dignity and decorum. No friend of southern Africa can doubt the overriding necessity that the negotiations currently in prospect between Mr Mandela and President de Klerk should go forward as urgently as possible, as the only hope of bringing lasting peace to that unhappy country.

Nevertheless, the outcome of the trial in Johannesburg must give rise to the most profound disquiet. Mrs Mandela is, after all, the wife of the deputy leader of the African National Congress, and her actions, even in her private life, must inevitably raise question marks over the judgement of those who are most closely associated with her, above all the deputy leader of the African National Congress Mr Nelson Mandela... lack of responsibility... gravest doubts about ability to govern... see what happens when these blacks are given an inch... can't trust them... running around with spears... leopard-skin accessories... only just down from trees... what did we always tell you?... serve 'em right... ha, ha, ha.

© TV's Charles Moore, Deputy Leader-writer, Telegraph National Congress ("Conrad Black Majority Rule")

Cannes Diary

Thursday

Crowds thronged to the Yugoslav pavilion for the long-awaited premiere of Mikhail Schlug's first feature, *Dead Strawberries*, which examines the childhood of a Yugoslavian writer whose father, a local communist official, hides his past from his son. A sensitive portrayal of an adolescent's rite of passage. Particularly memorable are the monochrome flashbacks to the tramshed, which are reminiscent of Beinhimov's later work, in particular *The Strawberry Trilogy*.

Friday

The Japanese entry for the Jury's coveted Bourdes Stiffe Award delighted an appreciative audience, including such notable *directeurs* as Jean-Luc Bergerac, Anatoly Fiat, and young Cuban *enfant terrible* Tomaso Sorz. ZZZZ by Karaoke examines the childhood of a Japanese writer whose father, an official at a labour camp, hides his past from his son. A sensitive portrayal of an adolescent's rite of passage. There was spontaneous applause for the scene in which the young Tojo discovers his father's ceremonial sword hanging on the wall of an old tramshed. Shot in black and white, seven hours hardly does this masterpiece justice.

Saturday

Cruised round the bars of the Cannes 'District Rouge' looking for action. *(Go back to the cinema. Ed.)*

Karaoke: Dazzling

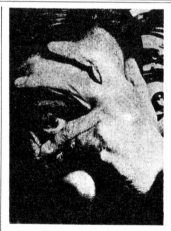

Werner Werner: Luminescent

Sunday

French Nouvelle Vague film noir *auteur* Marco Pierre Harvey received a standing ovation for the concluding part of his trilogy *Le Piat d'Or*. The film retraces the life of an elderly French writer back to his childhood in Vichy France, where his father was accused of collaborating with other filmmakers *(shurely 'the Germans'? Ed)* and tries to hide his past from his son. A sensitive evocation of an adolescent's "rites de passage". Particularly memorable is the sequence in which Thierry, played by newcomer Gerard Manliopkins, confronts his father in a deserted "shède du tram". An obvious contender for the critics' Complete Prix award.

Homme avec barbe

Monday

Britain's sole entry this year is by the young BFI graduate Chris Dull. Set against the backdrop of the Brixton riots, *I'm A White Liberal, Aren't Black Guys Great?* tells the story of an English film director whose father paid for him to go to film school. A sensitive evocation of an adolescent's terrible attempt to make a film.

(That's enough Cannes. Ed.)

SPOT THE MAJOR-BALL

Look carefully at this picture and then, before you fall asleep, put an X on the face of the man who is the most boring person in the photograph.

IMPORTANT
You are allowed only one attempt.

RULES
Members of the Cabinet and their families are not eligible to take part in this contest.

No prizes to be won

THE ALTERNATIVE VOICE

Deirdre Spart formerly Co-Chair Tufnell Park Socialist Workers "Ditch-the-Bitch" Action Group

It is totally sickening to see the Tory Party under their new leader acting totally typically in appointing an all-male Cabinet so that they feel safe in the all-boys-together world of public school misogyny and homophobia er... not one woman was chosen despite the fact that there are literally dozens of brilliant highly qualified women who could walk into the Cabinet tomorrow... women like... er... er... literally dozens of them who over the years have shown total callousness in their slavish adherence to the fascist Tory Government that has cut welfare child benefit hospitals under the most wimmin-hostile administration there has ever been led by none other than Mrs Thatcher the first woman Prime Minister who you have to hand it to her has shown women the way as Germaine Greer has pointed out (contd. p. 94)

"It's been ordered by Derek Hatton"

IN THE COURTS

Before Mr Justice Cocklecarrot.

The case of Mrs Edwina Currie v. Mr Donald Pixie, editor of the *Observer*.

SIR HARTLEY REDFACE QC *(for Mrs Currie)*: My Lord, it is my hideous duty to bring before this court one of the most loathsome and repulsive libels that has ever been perpetrated against any human being in the history of the world, viz that, on 23 April 1986, the "Eating Out" correspondent of the *Observer* newspaper, Miss Fay Mash, referred in her column to the experience of eating a "very hot curry" at the Amritsar Golden Temple restaurant, Uxbridge Road, west London, which had made her "feel distinctly unwell".

This disgraceful reference to my client was clearly designed to bring her political career to an immediate end. Any right-thinking person reading the phrase "hot curry" would have assumed, would he not, that my client was a libidinous and lascivious woman, the sort of woman who wears suspender belts beneath her skirts.

MR JUSTICE COCKLE-DRAKE: I wonder if it would help the jury here if we could have pictures?

SIR HARTLEY: I would merely ask you, ladies and gentlemen of the jury, to imagine it in your mind's eye. If I may pursue the question of meaning, My Lord, there can be little doubt that the words "hot curry" were intended to convey to the ordinary reader on the Clapham omnibus that my client was nothing better than a common prostitute, who was prepared at the drop of a hat to murder her children in order to further her political career.

MR CARTER-RUCK: Hooray, give us the money!

MR JUSTICE COCKA-LEEKIE: I must ask the solicitors for the plaintiff to restrain their greed, I mean their enthusiasm for justice, until after the jury have found the *Observer* guilty.

MR GEORGE CAR-PERSON QC *(for himself)*: My Lord, it was never the intention of my client, Mr Pixie, or his highly respected newspaper, the *Sunday Lonrho*, to cast aspersions in any way on Mrs Currie, who, as all of you will have seen, is a ghastly, publicity-seeking old hag who has only brought this action in the hopes of making a fast buck, which she no doubt intends to spend on buying expensive lingerie, probably including suspenders and black stockings.

MR JUSTICE COCKITUP: I do think you would assist your client's case, Mr Carperson, if you were to provide the jury with some pictures.

MR CARPARK: My Lord, I am sure Mrs Currie would be willing to strip off here and now, if she thought there were a few bob in it, or even a few votes. Let me sum up by saying that it has never been our intention to suggest that Mrs Currie is anything other than a conscientious and hard-working politician. But since she and her pimp over there *(points to distinguished grey-haired solicitor, who little deserves this distasteful slur on his good name)* have brought this trouble on themselves, I would merely ask that you jail both of them for a minimum of 20 years, before they murder us all in our beds.

MR JUSTICE COCKA-LOOPIE: Before I run over the evidence, can I just be absolutely sure that there is no photographic documentation in the bundles?

(Usher, Mr Cedric Fruitbowl, wakes up and shakes head disconsolately)

THE JUDGE: Members of the jury, when you come to the question of damages, which you assuredly will, as this is a tradition of English law in cases of libel, I must ask you to be modest and to award a sum which is only commensurate with the amount of money which, say, Mrs Currie might hope to earn in the course of an evening's work, were she a prostitute, which of course she is not.

MR EUGENE PUNTER *(foreman of the jury)*: You mean five grand, Your Honour?

JUDGE: Done.

(Exeunt lawyers to count their money)

NO. TEN TRILLION AND THIRTY-SIX

CLOUD NINE

HARP

THE IN-HOUSE MAGAZINE OF HEAVEN

Three billion Archangels axed as recession bites

BY OUR CELESTIAL STAFF ST PAUL FOOT
(CAMPAIGNING JOURNALIST OF THE MILLENNIUM)

ℙROOF that the recession is now the worst economic downturn in the past two million years came today with the news that God is to shed three billion middle-management archangels.

"This is only part of an across-the-board management shakeout which will eventually affect every tier of the celestial hierarchy," said Heavenly Spokesman Gabriel. "We are looking at a rationalisation programme which could involve redundancies among Cherubim, Seraphim, Thrones, Dominions, Powers, and even chanters of 'Holy, Holy, Holy'.

"People must stop thinking that they have got their jobs for eternity," said the Archangel.

The news of the cuts was greeted with dismay in the Celestial City, where many stocks were marked down sharply. Harps fell by a record two million points, and Haloes also eased, to finish well beneath their previous all-time low.

One leading cherub told me, off the record: "They say our father's house has many mansions but, I can tell you, we're not shifting any of them."

God Himself was unavailable for comment last night, preferring to remain invisible. But a seraph who had just received his redundancy notice spake forthwith, and said: "Lo, things must be serious up here if the Old Man is handing out the P45s. They will be telling us next that Marks & Spencers are laying people off."

Late News

Four Horseman of the Apocalypse to be slashed to One.

ST MATT

"I've just got the sackcloth and ashes"

Stop calling Major a twit now

says Norman Tebbit

THE Tory Party is in danger of tearing itself apart. And what is the so-called issue which is tempting so many of my fellow Conservatives to commit electoral suicide?

I will tell you. It is the leadership of our duly elected Prime Minister, Mr John Major. Well I say this.

Let's stop all this bickering and snickering now. Nothing at all is gained by speeches, television interviews and newspaper articles in the *Evening Standard* calling our Prime Minister dull, boring, colourless, incompetent, dithering, blithering, blathering, blethering (*Get on with it, Ed*) and unable to govern his way out of a paper bag.

So what if John Major is unable to make up his mind about anything? Does it really matter that he is the most useless prime minister we've ever had?

No. Nothing whatsoever is gained by pointing this out. Responsible members of the party should put an immediate veto on any further speeches suggesting that John Major is nothing but a C-stream prime minister in charge of a D-team cabinet.

OK, so he's not a patch on Mrs Thatcher. But what is the point of saying so when a general election may be only weeks away?

Isn't it time we all grew up? As an ex-chairman of the party, I call on all loyal Conservatives to give their one hundred per cent backing to this useless twit.

© *Evening Standard Why-Oh-Why*

Kenneth Baker.
Brilliant. Cunning. Psychotic.
Can he stop the killers?

18

the silence of the dogs

A *DAILY MAIL* HEALTH EXCLUSIVE

STRESS

TEN TELL-TALE SIGNS

1. Wears glasses
Eyes deteriorating, probably as a result of not understanding what he is reading.

2. Grey hair
Clear sign of cracking up.

3. Sore throat
Well-known symptom of mental instability.

4. Drowsiness
An early indicator of incompetence and insanity.

5. Called John
John is a name always associated with weak, hopelessly ineffectual leaders. Unlike, say, Maggie.

6. Not called Maggie
Conclusive evidence that he should resign at once.

7. Come back, Mrs T
The only way to restore this country to its former glory.

8. Major must go
See above.

9. Er…

10. That's It.

© *Paul Johnson and all other lunatic right-wingers who can't bear the fact that she's washed up.*

"Everybody down! This yoghurt's live!"

HELL!

NO. 94 • SEPT 28, 1990 • £1.00

EXCLUSIVE 48 PAGE INTERVIEW WITH SADDAM HUSSEIN: FAMILY MAN, DOG LOVER AND GOLFER

'The great leader opens his heart and his doors'

MY NEW LOVE BY PRINCESS TRACY OF LUXEMBOURG

EXCLUSIVE: SALMAN RUSHDIE SHOWS US ROUND HIS HIDEAWAY MAYFAIR PENTHOUSE

MICHAEL FISH: MY SECRET HEARTBREAK

DELLA FROM TV'S PERRY MASON TELLS OF HER DAUGHTER JASMINA'S NEW BABY ROXANNE – HEART WARMING PHOTOS

SIR ALASTAIR BURNET AT 90 – MORE HEART WARMING PHOTOS

PETER CARTER RUCK WELCOMES US ABOARD HIS LUXURY YACHT "The Libella"

HELLO!

NICHOLAS RIDLEY

AT STALLONE'S PARTY

Glamorous ex-Cabinet Minister "Nick Nick" Ridley was keen to shake off his anti-German image at Sly Stallone's party last week.

"It's rubbish," says the roguish ex-Department of Trade Supremo. "In fact, some of my best friends are Germans."

Looking relaxed and happy in the company of tennis superstar Steffi Graf, Nick winked at the *Hello* journalist and joked: "You're not Dominic Lawson, are you?"

Showbiz friends laughed heartily as "Nico" and Steffi proved that relationships between Germany and Britain are as cordial as ever.

"I'd better not mention Hitler, had I?" said the debonair chainsmoker. Steffi had to agree with him.

"Especially as he was in *Hello* last week!"

INTERVIEW: EVA BRAUNNOSE

DUDLEY MOORE'S 97th WIFE

Dud and the mystery blonde surprised in Cannes

"This time it's for real." So says the diminutive Hollywood heartthrob, star of *11*, *Arthur*, *12*, *Arthur II*, *13*, *Arthur Scargill* and *94½*.

Dudley has been seen constantly in the company of a leggy blonde who, friends say, is deeply in love with the much-married Mini-Romeo from Beverly Hills.

Dudley has come a long way

from his native Neasden. Today he earns $1 million a day and has been married 96 times.

"I've been in analysis for years, but finally I have found my plateau of contentment. I know who I am at last. I am Peter Cook." [H]

STEPHEN FRY'S SECRET LOVE

NOW THEY TALK OPENLY

The popular star of TV's *Mr Jeeves* has revealed that his celibate days are over.

The 37-year-old bachelor, renowned for his portrayal of the immortal butler Bertie Jeeves, said he was "over the moon" about his new friend.

She is vivacious socialite Lady Bubbles Rothermere. The happy couple asked us into their secret love nest in the South of France to share their happiness.

For once the eloquent Fry was speechless as he gazed with obvious rapture at his newfound love partner. And Bubbles could hardly stop talking about "the divine Stephen".

"Most young people today are so uncouth but Stephen is a real gentleman of the old school. He brings me a cup of tea and the *Telegraph* every morning and says 'Good morning, M'Lady. I trust you slept well.' "

Bubbling over in Fry Society!

INTERVIEWER: JOCK McCRAWLER

'She's awfully good, Penelope Keith, isn't she?'

LORD DENNING

THE NEW WOMAN IN HIS LIFE

"She is the apple of my eye, of that there is no mistaking." So says controversial hanging judge Lord Denning, 97, pictured with six-foot blonde Hollywood actress Brigitte Nielsen, 26.

The couple met on the set of Brigitte's latest movie, *Mutant Legal Hero Turtles III*. "It was love at first sight," says Sylvester Stallone's ex. "Despite the difference in our ages, Tom and I are seeing a lot of each other. He has a great sense of humour and his own career as a celebrity, which is very important.

"I wish we could be together more but if you are with a major legal star you have to accept that he will always be on TV giving interviews."

(Continued from page 37)
So we had the living room done in chintz sent out from Harrods. Mohammed is an old friend.
And you've got your handicap down to single figures?
That's right. I suppose having my own golf course has made a difference. We flew in the grass from Ireland and we've had to water it every day with a million gallons. Still, I was determined to be good enough to play with Roger Moore and Michael Caine in the Pro-Celebrity Iraqi Open in March.
What sort of dogs are these?
I am an animal lover and I have many dogs, including these longhaired Russian Bazookis. The black one is Prince and the pure white one is Snowy. Come here, Snowy. Good boy!
Do you ever cook yourself?
There's nothing I enjoy more than an evening in the kitchen. Fatima tells me I make a superb doner kebab, though sometimes I just open a can of baked beans if it is only me.
And do you enjoy television?
Indeed I do. We have satellite and cable and I enjoy your British sense of humour. *Blackadder* is the favourite of the children but I prefer *To The Manor Born*.
I understand you do a lot of work for charity?
I only wish I had more time for that sort of thing. People in my position can do so much, I know.
Who do you most admire?
I think it is Mother Teresa, although if I had my time again it would have to be Jim Reeves. I am a great country fan and would love to bring the Grand Ol' Opry to Baghdad one day.

INTERVIEWER: NOSTRILLO DE BRUNEI

ANDREAS WHITTAM-SMITH

THE INDEPENDENT MILLIONAIRE – AN EXCLUSIVE INTERVIEW

Andreas, how long have you had this delightful Hollywood mansion?

Ramona and I first came to LA in 1989 when I was Guest of Honour at the International Newspaper Editor of the Year Convention.

Did you ever dream that one day you would live here?

I commute between Beverly Hills, my castle in Holstein-Pils, and my Belgravia flat. It's the only way to keep control over my empire. But it's more than just that, it's because I am one of nature's gypsies. I have to be on the move.

How do you keep yourself so wonderfully fit?

I have a gym here in the basement and at the *Independent*, as you know, we have a staff workout every lunch hour. I swim a lot, the pool here was designed for me by Matty Sy-monds Jr *(an Olympic coach)* and it's the most up-to-date in the world. I get my best ideas swimming. For example, when I was diving into the deep end I thought of launching a Sunday newspaper.

How much money have you got?

I am very wealthy, very wealthy indeed. But money is not important to me. The paper is what matters. The paper that the shares are printed on.

Do you have any plans for the future?

We are planning to launch a special Monday paper. Our market research indicates there is a demand for a new type of Monday newspaper for people who don't normally buy a paper on Monday. We've got a dummy. He's called Steven Glover. Ha ha ha.

Thank you Sir Andreas for giving us so much of your valuable time.

INTERVIEW: ALFREDO DE NEZBRUN

THE DUCHESS OF YORK

PROUDLY SHOWS US HER SMALLEST ROOM

"Although we call it the smallest room, in fact it's one of the largest," said the beautiful red-haired Duchess of York when she gave us an exclusive glimpse of the David Hicks designed Royal Toilet Complex at the Yorks' brand new Sunningdale theme mansion.

"I could spend hours in here," laughed the country's most popular Royal as she posed demurely *(continued next issue)* **H**

THE WEDDING OF JEFF BERNARD AND PRINCESS VODKA

There were over 2,000 guests at the Chapel of San Raphael in the Principality of Monaco when playboy millionaire Jeff Bernard married his sixth wife, the lovely Princess Vodka of Smirnoff, the 337th in line to the throne of Bulgaria.

The couple hope to settle in Jersey, where Jeff has bought a £6 million country estate complete with swimming pool, helicopter pad and private bar.

"My play is so successful now that I will never have to work again. Not that I ever did before," he added jokingly. "I would love to take my bride to meet my Soho friends, but the tax laws make it impossible."

Princess Vodka looked stunning in her Norman Balon designer trousseau.

"He is the sweetest man alive and we are very much in love. His wild days are over. From now on, the strongest thing he'll drink is a cup of tea." **H**

INTERVIEWER: BRUNO NOSE